IN HER FOOTSTEPS

Where Trailblazing Women Changed the World

CONT

ENTS

INTRODUCTION

The history of the world is filled with the names of men, and their stories are easy to find, adorning countless monuments. The landmarks of female achievement, on the other hand, are often not so simple to find. There might not always be a towering obelisk to mark their contribution, but look a little closer and you can find monuments to female educators, artists, activists, warriors and more all over the globe. Some are household names; others have been overlooked for too long. Great women don't always make the history books, unfortunately.

But in some places, renowned women have left an unmistakable imprint. This book celebrates their contribution through the ages. It is a collection of landmarks (large and small, obvious and hidden) that are dedicated to great women, as well as spaces where they have gone about their lifework, creating a trail for travellers who want to be inspired by what's possible when you won't take 'no' for an answer.

Inside these pages are advocates for Indigenous peoples, chanteuses, women's suffrage leaders, Olympic athletes, environmentalists, spies, pirates, queens who opposed colonial rule; athletes who excelled in their field, aviators and intrepid adventurers who set off into the unknown, scientists whose discoveries made history and activists who wouldn't accept an unjust status quo. In fact, our greatest challenge was the embarrassment of riches to choose from, and the impossibility of including every deserving figure, both from the annals of history and from the front pages of today's newspapers.

The women profiled have endowed vast swaths of land as environmental preserves, spoken truth to power, marched and organised and protested, often at great risk and with fatal consequences, holding fast to their ideals even when it cost them their lives. Equally, they have written books, poems and songs that reflect back reader's own experiences, creating a literary treasure trove and, in the case of Murasaki Shikibu, originating the first novel. Some have marched against empire, whether in the form of Rome or a more recent incarnation. And when in power during eras that preferred male rule to a fault, they have strategised and conquered, often earning a scheming reputation as a result.

Often, their actions and beliefs have been circumscribed by the times they lived in, whether education activists who didn't take up the cause of suffrage or political leaders who allowed ethnic divisions to fester. Leaders of any gender identity are all subject to the same pressures and have personal biases. Nor can we know whether figures like Gentleman Jack would keep female pronouns today, outside of the constraints of their own era. Like any identity, that of woman (and feminist and queer) changes over time. It's no single monolithic thing; what's the fun in that?

This is an alternative travel guide to the world: one which documents the impact of incredible women from all walks of life. It shows a glimpse of the too-often forgotten influence of women past and present and celebrates their legacy. For the countless numbers of feminist heroes whom space didn't allow a proper tribute in these pages, we hope you'll find your own way to the streets named in their honour and the sites of their actions. May you always be inspired by the their example and emboldened to follow your own path.

ACTIVISTS

Church of San Agustin
LA POLA
Bogotá, Colombia

Turn on the TV in Colombia and you might catch a rerun of *La Pola*, a telenovela (soap opera) based on the life of Apolonia Salavarrieta, aka La Pola. Indeed, La Pola's life is worthy of the 200-episode run: as a young woman in Bogotá, the Colombian-born Salavarrieta spied on the Spanish Royalists, offering her services as a seamstress to their wives and daughters in order to collect intelligence on the generals' activities and plans. While La Pola was sewing buttons on shirt sleeves and mending hems, she listened carefully to the conversations around her, picking up details that she could communicate back to Colombian revolutionaries. Alongside her lover and collaborator, Alejo Sabaraín, La Pola was ultimately arrested as a traitor and sentenced to death by firing squad. Although she was instructed to turn her back for the execution, she bravely turned to face the shooters. According to the records, her last words were powerful: 'I have more than enough courage to suffer this death and a thousand more', she said. 'Do not forget my example'. She was buried at the convent of San Agustín in the Bogotá neighbourhood of La Candelaria. The day of her death, 14 November, was later chosen as the Day of the Colombian Woman. La Pola's face also appears on Colombian currency and postage stamps.

🔹 Born in 1795 and killed in 1817, La Pola was only 22 at the time of her death.

Belmont-Paul House

ALICE PAUL

Washington, DC, USA

'There will never be a new world order until women are a part of it.'

What's now known as the Belmont-Paul House was the final headquarters of the National Woman's Party (NWP), established in 1916 by Alice Paul (1885-1977). Paul was frustrated with the slow tactics of the National American Woman Suffrage Association and wanted to push harder for a constitutional amendment allowing women the right to vote. Her NWP was a more radical organisation, and kept detailed records on members of Congress for more effective lobbying. Alice Paul, Lucy Burns, Dorothy Day and other members were determined to convince

President Woodrow Wilson to back the proposed amendment. They marched in front of the White House with banners, the first time any group had dared picket the president's house. Among the objects you can see here: a commemorative suffrage trowel (because of course!), Elizabeth Cady Stanton's chair, Susan B Anthony's desk and the 'Congressional Card File/Deadly Political Index', a collection of detailed notes from meetings the NWP had with members of Congress. This kind of activist lobbying seems commonplace today, but it was an unheard-of tactic back then.

📍 The Belmont-Paul House is located right next to the Hart Senate Office Building (which has seen its own protests over the years).

Plaza de Mayo

MOTHERS OF THE DISAPPEARED

Buenos Aires, Argentina

Every Thursday in Buenos Aires, the Madres (Mothers) of Plaza de Mayo march around the square's obelisk. Some wear handkerchiefs on their silver hair, some hold banners showing the faces of their missing children, others carry signs: 'Ni olvido, ni perdón' (We'll never forgive, we'll never forget) and 'Memoria, verdad y justicia' (Memory, truth and justice). They've been marching weekly since 1977, demanding justice for children who disappeared during Argentina's military dictatorship. The nationwide nightmare of 1976–1983 began when a right-wing military junta overthrew Isabel Perón, president of Argentina. In the name of 'national reorganisation', the military government started rounding up guerrillas as well as journalists, students, writers and anyone suspected to stand in opposition to the regime. Human rights organisations estimate that as many as 40,000 people (known as desaparecidos, or the disappeared) were kidnapped by the military, thrown into clandestine detention and executed. The Madres originally united to seek information about the whereabouts of their children. Early on, it was dangerous to congregate in public: indeed, one of the founders, Azucena Villaflor, was captured and killed by the government. But as the disappearances continued, the Madres grew in number and in collective outrage. While some military leaders were later convicted of genocide, many of the Madres still don't know what happened to their family members — and they go on marching every Thursday, demanding answers.

📍 Plaza de Mayo is in downtown Buenos Aires, easily accessible by metro and bus and not far from the country's presidential palace.

12

'People always say that I didn't give up my seat because I was tired, but that isn't true. I was not tired physically...No, the only tired I was, was tired of giving in.'

Montgomery Bus Stop

ROSA PARKS

Alabama, USA

When she refused to give up her bus seat to a white man in 1955 Montgomery, Rosa Parks became a central figure in the US civil rights movement's fight against segregation. Her actions served as the catalyst for the year-long Montgomery bus boycott as well as later protests of civil disobedience that would come to define the movement. Rosa Parks' activism continued throughout her life – she established the Rosa and Raymond Parks Institute for Self Development to support youths overlooked by other social programs, and actively advocated for housing equality and criminal justice reform. She regularly donated her speaking fees to civil rights organisations around the country and was a recipient of the Presidential Medal of Freedom, the Congressional Gold Medal and the NAACP's Spingarn Medal. To trace her steps through history, visit the Montgomery bus stop that helped ignite the civil rights movement. Then head to the Rosa Parks Museum to learn more about the boycott's importance in the civil rights struggle.

📍 Montgomery is an essential stop for anyone interested in learning about the US civil rights movement. Visit the Dexter Avenue Parsonage (the home of Martin Luther King Jr and Coretta Scott King) and the Legacy Museum.

Florence Nightingale Museum

FLORENCE NIGHTINGALE

London, England

'I attribute my success to this: I never gave or took an excuse.'

The name of Florence Nightingale (1820-1910) is so widely known that it sometimes overshadows her actual work. Step in the museum devoted to her life and legacy, lodged in St Thomas' Hospital on the banks of the Thames facing the Houses of Parliament. The collection is not extensive, but it's personal and powerful. As you read Florence's letters, hear her voice in an original 1890 recording, and see her medicine chest, famous Turkish lantern lamp and pet owl Athena (now stuffed), which travelled everywhere in her pocket, slowly you can piece together the puzzle of this most extraordinary and selfless of women.

Named after the city of her birth, at age 17

Nightingale bucked the conventions of her upper-middle-class Victorian upbringing to pursue her 'God-given' vocation of nursing. She became a heroine following her role in the Crimean War. Appalled by the fact that more men were dying in infection-riddled hospitals than on battlefields, she led a team of nurses there to work day and night saving lives – hence the 'Lady of the Lamp' nickname. With ideas well ahead of her time, she revolutionised nursing, creating the Nightingale Home and Training School for Nurses.

The museum is just behind Waterloo station, on the Bakerloo, Jubilee and Northern underground lines.

Greenwich Village

MARGARET SANGER

Manhattan, USA

Pre-WWI New York City was the right place at the right time for Margaret Sanger (1879-1966). The city's leftist circles sparked her passion for social justice and gave her the courage to speak out about women's health. For Margaret Sanger, social justice meant birth control. Her own mother died at 49, having been pregnant 18 times and having given birth to 11 children. In her work as a nurse in the slums of New York City, Sanger saw firsthand the despair that unplanned babies caused. Women were dying from self-induced abortions and families were living in poverty from too many mouths to feed. Interestingly, while Margaret championed sex education and contraception, she felt abortion was reprehensible. Reducing the need for abortions was one of her major motivators for educating women about birth control and providing them access to it.

Sanger founded the American Birth Control League in 1921 with the philosophy that children be 'conceived in love' with a 'conscious desire' of their mothers to give birth. This organisation eventually evolved into Planned Parenthood. Margaret would continue to push for women's right to birth control throughout the world for the rest of her life. The building that was home to her Birth Control Clinical Research Bureau, at 17 West 16th St, is now privately owned, and the area has changed since her time, but the facade still stands, along with her former apartment at 4 Perry St.

📍 You can also check out Margaret Sanger Square in nearby Noho.

© Bettmann / Getty Images

Library of Congress

KATHERINE DUNHAM

Washington, DC, USA

A student of anthropology – she got a doctorate in the subject – Katherine Dunham (1909–2006) is deservedly well known for her dancing and choreography, but her social activism was a constant throughout her career as well. A star of the stage, she formed her own dance company devoted to African American and Afro-Caribbean dance. Alongside her artistry, she tirelessly championed the rights of African Americans; as early as 1944 she refused to return to Louisville, Kentucky, if it wouldn't desegregate its theatres, and her 1951 *Southland* dance is an anti-lynching piece. In 1992 she went on a hunger strike to protest US government treatment of Haitian refugees. No wonder Dunham's archive is held within the prestigious Library of Congress.

📍 The Katherine Dunham Collection at the Library of Congress preserves materials documenting 'the extraordinary journey of a woman who changed the face of American modern dance'.

© picture alliance / Getty Images

University of Groningen

ALETTA JACOBS

Groningen, Netherlands

Aletta Jacobs (1854-1929) was the first woman in the Netherlands to earn a medical degree. Throughout her life she was a tireless advocate for women's rights, social justice and pacifism. A woman before her time, she promoted the use of birth control, a stance unheard of in the Victorian era, and in 1880 she established the first birth control clinic in Amsterdam. Denied the right to vote as a woman, she founded the Woman Suffrage Alliance (Vereeniging voor Vrouwenkiesrecht) and stayed at its helm until 1919 when they were victorious, achieving the vote for all Dutch women.

📍 A bust at the University of Groningen, where Jacobs studied, commemorates her and all of her achievements.

Val-Kill Cottage

ELEANOR ROOSEVELT

Hyde Park, USA

'I have a firm belief in the ability and power of women to achieve the things they want to achieve.'

There's nothing remarkable about disliking your mother-in-law. What is remarkable, however, is when it's the impetus for building a house of your own on your husband's family estate. As grand as their home in Hyde Park was, Eleanor Roosevelt (1884-1962) disliked 'retreats' to Springwood, chafing under Sara Roosevelt's control. Luckily, there was room for both women on the 181-acre property. In 1924, with a lifetime lease from her husband, Eleanor and two friends built Stone Cottage as a residence. She named the area Val-Kill, a loose translation of the Dutch for waterfall and stream.

Two years later the group erected another building to serve as the home of Val-Kill Industries, an idea Eleanor had for area farmers to earn extra income. Known more for her passion for human rights and her radical belief in women's ability to do things than her interest in homemaking, Eleanor's Val-Kill is basic in its interiors. Even so, the Roosevelts happily entertained friends, family, and world leaders there. At Val-Kill, Eleanor flourished, gathering like-minded people to discuss and solve social issues of the day. In 1936 Val-Kill Industries closed, its legacy living on as a model for New Deal recovery programs. Eleanor went on to remodel the big building into a home for herself. Val-Kill would be the only place she ever felt truly at home, as well as a base to host the dignitaries she worked with in her role at the UN.

Admission is by guided tour only. New York's Hudson Valley has endless historic homes to visit; try Hyde Park's Vanderbildt Mansion.

Epsom Downs Racecourse

EMILY WILDING DAVISON

Surrey, England

Was she trying to get herself killed by stepping in front of King George V's horse at the 1913 Derby? Was she actually attempting to attach something symbolically to the bridle and had no wish to pay the ultimate sacrifice? Prominent suffragette Emily Wilding Davison (1872-1913) divided public opinion in her life, as well as in the protest that ended in her death. But that act before the King – brave or foolhardy – was the one that really swayed consensus in favour of granting women the vote, which was done in two laws in 1918 and 1928. The plaque commemorating Davison at the racecourse, unveiled in 2013, certainly marks one of the most important sites in the history of women's suffrage.

➡ The nearest train station to the racecourse is Tattenham Corner, with trains half-hourly via Purley to London.

© ErnestoGravelpond / Alamy Stock Photo

© Jane Barlow / Getty Images

Drumchapel High School

AMAL AZZUDIN

Glasgow, Scotland

A leading voice in activism for refugees, Somali-born Amal Azzudin (born 1990) came to Scotland as a refugee in 2000 with her family. When one of her schoolmates was swept up in 2015 dawn raids on local asylum seekers by UK Border Force, Amal and six schoolmates formed the Glasgow Girls and began a series of protests to raise awareness of the human rights of refugees. Visitors to Drumchapel in Glasgow can see the school where their activism began.

⬅ Protests are still held at Dungavel immigration centre in South Lanarkshire, less than an hour from Glasgow.

Puerto Madero

ALICIA MOREAU DE JUSTO

Buenos Aires, Argentina

In the late '90s, dozens of streets in Buenos Aires' waterfront neighbourhood of Puerto Madero were named after notable Argentine women, including human rights activist Azucena Villaflor, writer Victoria Ocampo and Cecilia Grierson, Argentina's first female doctor. Alicia Moreau de Justo (1885–1986), after whom a major avenue is named, is particularly notable. Appointed as a delegate to the 1919 International Workers' Congress in Washington, DC, she crossed the Andes on a mule to make it to Santiago, Chile, where she boarded a ship north to join the women's suffrage movement.

© mikecesar / Getty Images

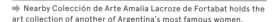

➡ Nearby Colección de Arte Amalia Lacroze de Fortabat holds the art collection of another of Argentina's most famous women.

© Grand Warszawski / Shutterstock

Pawiak Prison Museum

IRENA SENDLER

Warsaw, Poland

Polish social worker Irena Sendler (1910–2008) belonged to Konrad Żegota Committee (the Council to Aid Jews) and with the group worked to save 2500 children from Warsaw's ghetto. Her efforts led to her imprisonment in Pawiak Prison, where the Gestapo held 100,000 prisoners during the war. The prison was blown up by the Germans in 1944, but a mangled chunk of gateway and three detention cells survive. A Nobel Peace Prize nominee, Sendler is honoured by Holocaust Remembrance Center Yad Vashem and received Poland's Order of the White Eagle.

⬅ A joint ticket covers admission here as well as to the Mausoleum of Struggle & Martyrdom and the Warsaw Citadel.

Southport Island

RACHEL CARSON

Maine, USA

Rachel Carson (1907–1964) didn't have the financial or personal freedom that is often required for women to fulfil their destinies. And yet, she did it anyway. The Great Depression put an early end to Carson's academic career, but she never stopped discovering and observing the world around her and, most important, writing about it in a way that influenced public policy for generations. Her passionate environmentalism grew out of a deep connection to nature, from her birthplace of rural Pennsylvania to coastal Maine, where she settled later in life. Thanks to the success of her writing, where Carson blended science with prose that made subjects like sea life fascinating to even the most 'indoorsy' of readers, Carson was able to build Silverledges, her beloved cottage on Southport Island, Maine. Carson built the cottage with the sea in mind, orienting its big windows to maximise her views of the ocean, seals and whales. Silverledges was open to all of Carson's friends and family, including her grandnephew Roger. Carson adopted Roger after his mother died and the two spent thousands of happy hours exploring the tide pools around the cottage. She channelled this love for the natural world when she wrote *Silent Spring*, her 1962 magnum opus against pesticides.

📍 Visitors can breathe in the peace of Silverledges by renting out the cottage at a weekly rate. The island is accessible via swing bridge from US 1 North. Also off US 1 is the Rachel Carson National Wildlife Refuge.

> 'There is no logic that can be superimposed on the city; people make it, and it is to them, not buildings, that we must fit our plans.'

Washington Square Park

JANE JACOBS

Manhattan, USA

Brick rowhouses and prewar tenement buildings line the streets of Manhattan's historic Greenwich Village. Now home to many of the city's best restaurants, most fashionable boutiques and its largest private university, it was once the epicentre of 20th-century American counterculture, from Abstract Expressionist painters to anti-war protesters to groundbreaking jazz musicians who played in clubs like the Village Vanguard, where you can still catch a show today. At the middle of it all is the urban oasis of Washington Square Park, where you can find the Washington Square Arch along with students, dogs and, in the summer, pianists playing baby grands.

Only a short walk from Washington Square lies the small red rowhouse at 555 Hudson St where writer and activist Jane Jacobs lived in the 1950s and 60s, when she pioneered a new approach to urban planning in her landmark work *The Death and Life of Great American Cities*. For Jacobs, the ideal city was not ordered and regimented, but crowded, vibrant and diverse, just like her neighbourhood in Manhattan. When city planner Robert Moses proposed a Lower Manhattan Expressway that would have demolished a wide swath of the Village including Washington Square, Jacobs led the fight to save her beloved neighbourhood – and succeeded.

Each year on the first weekend in May, the Jane's Walk Weekend hosts guided neighbourhood tours across the globe in her honour.

Newington Green

MARY WOLLSTONECRAFT

London, England

Though she died at the age of only 38 in 1797, days after giving birth to future author of *Frankenstein* Mary Shelley, Mary Wollstonecraft left a rich heritage as one of the spiritual founders of the feminist movement. Her treatise *Vindication of the Rights of Women* argued that the perceived intellectual inferiority of women was a result of their inferior education. Born in East London, Wollstonecraft had an early and brutal education in the subjugation of women, lying outside her mother's bedroom to protect her from her father's drunken anger. As well as experiencing and writing about the French Revolution,

Wollstonecraft founded a girls' boarding school on Newington Green, where she embedded herself in a community of radicals and dissenters. Her life was bravely unconventional: she had two children outside marriage and wrote about female sexuality and desire. Visitors to the Green in search of Mary, mother of feminist free thought, can see a plaque on the school building, and a monochrome graffiti portrait of her down the side of the nearby Unity Chapel. A long-running campaign to erect a statue of Mary by the artist Maggi Hambling on the site aims to help redress the sad fact that more than 90% of London's statues depict men.

Newington Green sits on the borders of Islington and Hackney, on the route of the #73 bus.

© benedek / Getty Images

La Casa de Libertad

JUANA AZURDUY

Sucre, Bolivia

Fierce freedom fighter Juana Azurduy (1780–1862) was born in the Bolivian region of Chuquisaca (now Sucre) into a well-off family, but from an early age rebelled against convention and became an ally of the indigenous revolutionary movement. In the fight for Bolivian independence, Azurduy earned the title of lieutenant colonel and commanded an army of thousands of men. She was a sharpshooter, a mother of five who left the battlefield to give birth to her fourth child before returning to capture the Spanish flag, and a fluent speaker of indigenous languages. Although she died in poverty and was buried in a communal grave, a room in the constitutional capital's House of Freedom (La Casa de la Libertad) is dedicated to Azurduy in recognition of her heroic leadership.

📍 Stroll through or take a picnic lunch to Parque Bolívar, Sucre's largest park.

© Zack Frank / Shutterstock

Harriet Tubman Underground Railroad
National Historical Park

HARRIET TUBMAN

Maryland Eastern Shore, USA

Harriet Tubman (1822-1913) was the best-known
conductor of the Underground Railroad and one
of the most important human rights activists
in US history. Not only did she lead nearly 70
enslaved people to freedom, she also served as
a nurse, and eventually a spy, for the Union Army
during the Civil War. In 1863 she became the first
woman to lead a Civil War armed assault, a raid on
plantations along the Combahee River that freed
750 people from slavery. After the war, Tubman
became involved in the fight for women's suffrage
and established a home for the elderly. Tubman's
heroism still inspires, and those wishing to delve
into her legacy will find eastern Maryland – where
she was born, escaped from slavery and rescued
many – a treasure trove. To learn more about her
courageous accomplishments, head to Church
Creek's Harriet Tubman Underground Railroad
National Historic Park. The site has exhibits about
her life and is the first stop on the Harriet Tubman
Byway, a 125-mile driving tour of 36 sites related to
Tubman's work and the Underground Railroad.

📍 The historical park is only two hours drive from Washington, DC;
combine your visit with a day at the National Museum of African
American History and Culture.

Reserva Biológica Opalaca

BERTA CÁCERES

Intibucá, Honduras

Berta Cáceres was born in 1971 within the Lenca community, the largest indigenous group in Honduras. As a young woman, she became a student activist, co-founding a social and environmental organisation to protect Lenca territory and its people against the rising threat of destructive mining and construction projects. In 2006 Cáceres initiated a grassroots campaign to stop the building of the Agua Zarca Dam – a joint project between a Honduran company and a massive Chinese-owned dam developer – on the Gualcarque River, which originates in the Reserva Biológica Opalaca in Intibucá and was long considered sacred by the Lenca. The dam wouldn't only obstruct the flow of the river: it would also have cut off the supply of water, food and medicine to the indigenous people on its shores. After years of struggle and the involvement of several international organisations, Cáceres and her supporters succeeded in their efforts to have the dam's construction contract terminated. For her humanitarian and environmental work, Cáceres was awarded the 2015 Goldman Prize. But Cáceres was in trouble, especially after the 2009 Honduran coup d'état: along with other human rights activists, she faced ongoing intimidation from the military and various threats on her life. She was assassinated at home in March 2016, leaving behind four children, her husband and a strong legacy of activism.

The remote biological reserve isn't easily accessible: to get there, rent a jeep and drive from Tegucigalpa (if political conditions allow).

'My grandfather said to me, you have to first love yourself, and spread it around.'

Redfern

MUM SHIRL

Sydney, Australia

Tireless activist and social worker Colleen Shirley Perry, aka Mum Shirl (1921–1998), was a Wiradjuri woman who spent most of her life in Redfern, Sydney's sometimes-troubled inner-city Aboriginal precinct. Shirl began to visit and support Aboriginal prisoners when one of her brothers was incarcerated. Seeing that her visits were a huge support for prisoners, she kept visiting. When Corrective Services workers asked about her relationship to the prisoners, she would reply 'I'm his mum', which is how she earned the name 'Mum Shirl'. Mum Shirl played a lead role in establishing the Aboriginal Legal Service, the Aboriginal Medical Service and the Aboriginal Tent Embassy, the long-running protest occupation established on the lawn outside Old Parliament House in Canberra since 1972. She had a reputation for opening her home to anyone in need, and by the end of her life she had raised over 60 children. A plaque in her honour at Redfern's St Vincent De Paul Catholic Church reads 'In celebration of the life of Mum Shirl, the black saint of Redfern who gave aid and comfort to all who asked'.

● While visiting Redfern, stop into 107 Projects, a hive of art-making and community creativity at 107 Redfern St.

Parliament Square

MILLICENT GARRETT FAWCETT

London, England

With a look of quiet determination, the face of Millicent Garrett Fawcett (1847-1929) is cast in bronze in London's Parliament Square. The statue's hands hold aloft a banner that reads 'Courage calls to courage everywhere', a call to arms against inequality. Among dozens of statues of political and intellectual heavyweights on the square – like Abraham Lincoln and Nelson Mandela – Fawcett is the only woman represented. Remembered for her inexhaustible work campaigning for women's voting rights, Fawcett's organisational skills gave a boost to the suffragist movement, which favoured nonviolent activism (in contrast to dramatic protests by the suffragettes). In 1897 Fawcett took the helm of the democratic National Union of Women's Suffrage Societies, accelerating political support for equal voting rights.

Parliament Square today is equal parts tourist hot spot and political lightning rod. On any given day, tourists can be seen milling about, angling for a perfect shot of Westminster Abbey or Big Ben. Protests also gather here, so it's fitting that the bronze statue of Fawcett fixes her challenging gaze towards parliament. Fashioned by Turner Prize–winning British artist Gillian Wearing, the sculpture is also Parliament Square's first statue created by a woman artist. The statue was unveiled on the centenary of 1918's Representation of the People Act, which granted some women aged over 30 the right to vote in the UK. Today, the latest wave of feminists take selfies with the statue.

📍 Devoted admirers of Fawcett can also seek out her former home, marked by a blue plaque at 2 Gower St.

'Only if we understand, will we care. Only if we care, will we help. Only if we help shall all be saved.'

Gombe Stream National Park

JANE GOODALL

Gombe, Tanzania

Few people have impacted how we define humanity as much as Jane Goodall. In 1958 Dr Louis Leakey chose her to lead chimpanzee research at Gombe National Park, Tanzania, before she even had a university degree; this was unprecedented and yet, decades later, it's obvious that the animal-loving young woman from London (she was only 26 when research began in 1960) was the best choice for the job. Gombe is a small but incredibly biodiverse region of steep valleys, grassland and jungle that's accessible only by boat. Rather than set herself physically and emotionally at a distance from the chimps (the standard for animal research), Goodall slowly became accepted by the animals and developed close bonds with them that led to astounding observations. What she saw included tool-making, hunting for meat and even war in the primates' society. She found so many similarities between chimps and humans that it became

necessary for the scientific community to re-evaluate what distinguishes humans from the rest of the animal kingdom.

But while her decades of groundbreaking chimpanzee research are best known, Goodall is as legendary for her conservation work. She saw early on that her beloved chimps were threatened by habitat destruction and illegal trafficking, leading her to found the Jane Goodall Institute to encourage individual action to help save the natural world. She's also worked with various animal rights groups, and her organisation Roots & Shoots brings young people together to work on environmental and conservation issues. Even in her 80s, she's on the road ~300 days per year raising awareness and money for her causes.

📍 Visitors to Gombe can see Jane's old chimp-feeding station, the viewpoint on Jane's Peak and Kakombe Waterfall.

Museo Manuela Sáenz

MANUELA SÁENZ

Quito, Ecuador

Born in Quito, Manuela Sáenz (1795-1856) married a wealthy Englishman in 1817. But it was her eight-year love affair with Venezuelan political leader Simón Bolívar – a relationship that began when she left her husband in 1822 – that shaped her as a revolutionary. Known in South America as *El Libertador* (the Liberator), Bolívar led Venezuela, Bolivia, Ecuador, Colombia, Peru and Panama in the fight for independence from Spain. And Sáenz, his lover of eight years, worked closely at his side, blocking an attempt on Bolívar's life in Bogotá in 1828 and helping him to escape, not to mention leading the battle for women's rights. Bolivár nicknamed her 'la Libertadora del Libertador' (the Liberator of the Liberator); in Ecuador and throughout Latin America, she's celebrated as a heroine of independence. In old paintings, she's often pictured riding horseback in men's clothing, an image that's made her a popular icon among feminist groups. At the museum erected in her honour in Ecuador's capital, located in a colonial house in Old Quito, visitors can read the love letters exchanged by Bolívar and Sáenz.

📍 The museum is located in Quito's Old Town within easy walking distance of many historic attractions.

Ida B Wells House

IDA B WELLS

Chicago, USA

Journalist, editor, activist and educator Ida B Wells was a civil rights pioneer who vocally fought against prejudice, hate and inequality during the end of the 19th and beginning of the 20th centuries. After a friend was lynched, Wells began what is often regarded as the first anti-lynching campaign, writing a scathing editorial in her paper, *The Memphis Free Speech and Headlight*; she received violent threats after its publication, and soon left Memphis. She began travelling to research other lynchings across the country, give lectures and lead protests against lynching.

In addition to her anti-lynching work, Wells also was an active supporter of women's suffrage, the founder of the National Association of Colored Women and a founding member of the NAACP. Wells was a vehement opponent of segregation (her voice led to major change in the Chicago school system), and she later ran for Illinois State Senate. Her Chicago home at 3624 S Dr Martin Luther King Jr Drive is a local landmark. The house is a private residence and not open to the public, but is marked with a placard that serves as a reminder of her fierce legacy.

To learn even more about her life, you can also visit the Ida B Wells-Barnett Museum in her hometown of Holly Springs, Mississippi, located on the property where she was born.

Parque Nacional Pumalín Douglas Tompkins

KRISTINE TOMPKINS

Chaitén, Chile

In 2019 Kristine Tompkins finalised the largest land donation in history as she and the Tompkins Conservation trust made the formal gift of Parque Pumalín and Parque Patagonia to the Chilean state. A UN patron of protected areas (and a former Patagonia CEO), Tompkins is an environmentalist and philanthropist second to none. She and her husband Doug – who tragically died in a kayaking accident in 2015 – began working on the Pumalín Project in 1991, when the Tompkinses, originally from California, acquired the 17,000-hectare Reñihué Field to protect the native virgin temperate forest from logging.

Parque Pumalín eventually grew in size to over 402,000 hectares, extending from the Andes to the misty Pacific coast fjords, and comprising volcanoes, waterfalls, centuries-old alerce trees and other native vegetation and wildlife. Its

location at the top of the Carretera Austral in northern Patagonia make it a favourite stop for visitors to enjoy the pristine natural environment. Parque Nacional Pumalín Douglas Tompkins and the other big Tompkins project, Parque Nacional Patagonia, are now the crown jewels of the Chilean national park system and highlights of the over 2700km (1700 mile) Route of Parks, assuring the preserve Tompkins created with so much love will belong to all.

'We have a moral imperative now in the face of climate change - in the face of everything we know - to get out of bed and really put the hammer down and fight for those places you love. You can't expect that someone else is going to do it.'

Trekkers here can hike glaciers and the rim of an active volcano.

Museo del Templo Mayor

RIGOBERTA MENCHÚ

Mexico City, Mexico

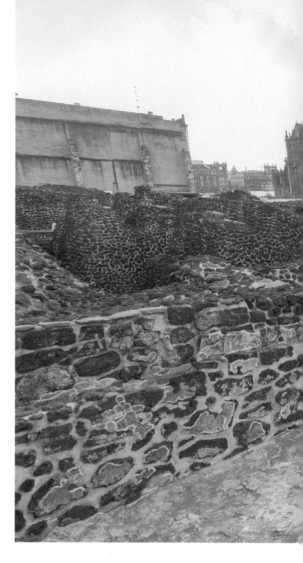

Guatemalan human rights activist Rigoberta Menchú won the Nobel Peace Prize in 1992. But she didn't bring the medal or certificate back to her native country: she entrusted her prize to the Mexican government, where it's been on display ever since at the Aztec Templo Mayor Museum in Mexico City. The peace medal, Menchú said at the time, would remain in a state of vigil until human rights conditions improve in Guatemala.

The decision made a strong statement to her country – one that reflected Menchú's drive to improve the lives of indigenous people. Born into a poor family in 1959, part of the k'iche' branch of the Maya culture, Menchú was involved in activism from an early age, helping her father educate people in rural Maya communities about their rights. She later became involved with women's rights, then began organising against human rights violations by the Guatemalan military during the country's long civil war. Along with her parents, she was accused

of participating in guerrilla activities. After her brother and mother were arrested, tortured and killed by the Guatemalan army, Menchú escaped to Mexico.

From her new home, she continued to organise indigenous resistance in Guatemala, calling for justice when the civil war was over: thanks to her efforts, in 2006, Spanish courts extradited seven members of Guatemala's military government on charges of genocide. Menchú was named a Unesco Goodwill Ambassador and co-founded the Nobel Women's Initiative along with five other female Nobel Peace Laureates representing North America, South America, Europe, the Middle East and Africa. Although death threats followed her on various attempts to return to her country, she ran for president of Guatemala in 2007 and 2011.

📍 Templo Mayor is located in the historic centre of Mexico City, steps from the central Zócalo plaza.

© Christian Heinegg / Alexander Turnbull Library

Auckland Harbour Bridge

WHINA COOPER

Auckland, New Zealand

Although Dame Whina Cooper was made a CBE for her activism on behalf of the Māori, she said of the recognition that 'I am the wearer, to show that if some can get to these heights, we all can...I came out of the teatree, out of a nikau hut, out of the country'. Her most famous moment was at the head of the 1975 land march protest: nearly 80 years old, she led this *hīkoi* (protest march) 1000km from Te Hapua to New Zealand's capital of Wellington by way of Auckland Harbour Bridge, demanding the Treaty of Waitangi's land rights be respected. She was dubbed *Te Whaea o te Motu*, the Mother of the People, for her tireless efforts. Born in 1895 and living until age 98, her career as a community leader spanned six decades. The hīkoi she organised in 1975 continues to inspire other actions to bring attention to Māori rights.

 Bridge climbs and bungee jumps are on the Auckland Harbour Bridge's list of non-protest offerings.

Roseland Theatre

VIOLA DESMOND

New Glasgow, Canada

Halifax native Viola Desmond, who founded and managed her own beauty school and cosmetics company, advanced Canada's quest for civil rights after her car broke down and she decided to kill time at the movies. In 1946 Desmond sat in a 'whites only' section of New Glasgow's Roseland Theatre and refused to move to the balcony designated for black patrons. While Canada had no official racial segregation laws, many businesses (including the Roseland) unofficially required people of different races to be separated. Desmond's act of civil disobedience became a catalyst for Canada's civil rights movement.

To recognise her role, in 2018, Viola Desmond became the first woman to be pictured on Canada's $10 bill.

María Orosa Avenue

MARIA OROSA

Manila, Philippines

A pharmaceutical genius with a humanitarian streak, María Orosa (1893–1945) dedicated her life to lifting women and families out of poverty. In the early 1900s she stowed away on a boat set for the US, where she went on to earn both a bachelor's and master's degree in pharmaceutical chemistry from the University of Washington. Her scientific education informed all of her food advocacy work, and in the 1920s she returned to the Philippines to establish a nationwide campaign that improved the condition of women in barrios by teaching them meal planning, food preservation and poultry raising. As a result of working with these poor communities, she invented a clay pot oven that could function in absence of electricity or gas.

During WWII she joined the guerilla forces and helped save thousands of Filipinos, Americans and other nationals held in Japanese concentration camps – smuggling a powdered soybean she created (now the basis of Soyalac) to malnourished prisoners. She refused to leave the war effort and died in Manila when she was hit by shrapnel during a skirmish. Apart from her humanitarian work, Orosa invented the food staple and cultural mainstay banana ketchup, which she devised during a tomato shortage when bananas were abundant and cheap. A constant innovator, she also pioneered the process to create Filipino wines from cashew and guava and developed starch and flour from banana and cassava.

📍 The major street in Manila named after Maria Orosa (pictured below) ends at Jose Rizal Park.

İztuzu Beach

JUNE HAIMOFF

Dalyan, Turkey

Dalyan is a typically laid-back Mediterranean farming-turned-tourist town, which attracts visitors from all over Europe to its beach and the millennia-old acropolis at Kaunos. Back in 1975 it attracted Briton June Haimoff, who arrived on her boat and set up house in a *baraka* (beach hut)

on İztuzu Beach, aka Turtle Beach. The beach's nickname gives a clue about what fate had in store for the lady fondly known as Kaptan (Captain), as does the sea turtles statue on Dalyan's main square: İztuzu is an important Mediterranean nesting site of the endangered *Caretta caretta* (loggerhead sea turtle). Haimoff soon found herself joining forces with environmentalists to nix the construction of an 1800-bed resort on the beach, and subsequently established the Sea Turtle Conservation Foundation.

The work of Kaptan June, for which she was awarded an MBE in 2011 at the age of 89, has made Dalyan a key conservation site for the loggerheads. Foundation initiatives have included giving out locally manufactured propeller guards to tour boats, and petitioning to stop unethical 'turtle-spotting' tours that attract the marine giants by feeding them unsuitable crab or chicken. A broader issue is habitat destruction by dams and tourist development along the Mediterranean coast, and İztuzu is now a protected area. A line of wooden stakes on the beach indicates off-limits nesting sites and nighttime visits are prohibited during summer, when the turtles nest. June's humble *baraka* is still here, and now forms part of the Sea Turtle Research, Rescue & Rehabilitation Centre. In the centre, visitors can see injured loggerhead and green turtles being treated before their return to the sea.

📍 İztuzu Beach is 13km (8 miles) south of Dalyan, served by regular minibuses in summer.

Central Park Mall

SOJOURNER TRUTH

Manhattan, USA

Sojourner Truth (1797–1883) began her life under the name Isabella, enslaved in Ulster County, New York, on a Dutch-speaking farm. She suffered and survived cruel abuse. Through this torment, Isabella sought solace in the forest, and she began having conversations with God. These helped steel her for escape, which she did in 1826, walking away, never to return. After escaping to freedom she spent the rest of her life as a women's rights activist and abolitionist.

She began living in New York City in 1828 and became a Pentecostal preacher, sharing her faith and rallying for African American and women's rights. She took the name Sojourner Truth in 1843. Truth became one of the most powerful voices in the fight for human rights in the 19th century. She fought against slavery and for land to give to the people who were freed. One of Sojourner Truth's most famous speeches, *Ain't I a Woman?*, became the rallying cry for a movement. Her increasing role in the women's suffrage movement brought her into contact with Elizabeth Cady Stanton and Susan B Anthony, and the three will be memorialised with a statue in Central Park's Mall.

The statue will be unveiled in Central Park's Mall (pictured below) in 2020, on the centennial of women achieving the right to vote in the US.

Gowalia Tank Maidan

ARUNA ASAF ALI

Mumbai, India

It was 1942, and the struggle for independence from the British was at full boil. At Gowalia Tank Maidan in Mumbai, Jawaharlal Nehru (later to become India's first prime minister) was expected to address a crowd of 10,000. Gandhi was to make an appearance. But at the last minute, a posse of policemen swept the speakers into jail. The crowd was fractious, on the cusp of violence. Undeterred, Aruna Asaf Ali walked into this thicket of friction, addressed the crowd from the stage and unfurled the Indian flag. 'Hardly had the flag been unfurled when the police lobbed tear-gas shells into the crowd,' remembered Ali. Police fired and eight people died; Ali went on to become Delhi's first elected mayor in 1958. The maidan (now renamed August Kranti Maidan) hosts a memorial to that day, a pink lotus on a column.

🌑 A ten-minute walk from the Kemps Corner junction, Gowalia Tank is easily accessible by public buses and taxi. The nearest railway station is Grant Road.

© Bill Perry / Shutterstock

Chamber of Deputies

ELVIA CARILLO PUERTO

Mexico City, Mexico

Born in the Yucatán in 1878, Elvia Carrillo Puerto – nicknamed 'La Monja Roja' (the Red Nun) – was a feminist pioneer. After marrying at age 13 and becoming a widow in her early twenties, Carrillo went on to found the country's first women's resistance league, in 1912. A decade later, alongside two other women, she was elected to the state legislature. Although she was shot at eight times during her campaign for Federal Deputy, and the Chamber of Deputies refused to seat her, Carillo never stopped fighting for women's rights. Thanks in part to her persistence, Mexican women won the right to vote in 1953.

🌑 Stop for tacos from one of the food vendors who set up their stands on downtown's pedestrianised streets nearby.

Mirabal Sisters House and Museum

MIRABAL SISTERS

Salcedo, Dominican Republic

Between 1924 and 1935, four daughters were born into the Dominican Republic's Mirabal family: Patria, Dedé, Minerva and Maria Teresa. As young women, they became involved in opposing the dictatorship of Rafael Trujillo, nicknamed *El Jefe* (the Boss). Trujillo's brutal military regime, responsible for many thousands of deaths, was in power for more than three decades. Minerva, Maria Teresa and Patria were active in the movement (Dedé, following her husband's wishes, steered clear of the resistance), founding a group named after the Fourteenth of June, the date of one of Trujillo's bloodiest massacres.

Nicknaming themselves *Las Mariposas* (the Butterflies), the sisters distributed information about the regime's victims and obtained guns and bombs to use in protest. Along with their husbands, who also participated in the movement, the three sisters were eventually captured and imprisoned. As Trujillo's dictatorship earned international notoriety, the women were released from incarceration. But the men were not. On 25 November 1960, the three sisters, accompanied by their driver, went to visit their husbands in prison. Trujillo's righthand man apprehended them on their way home: all three were assassinated.

Dedé lived to tell the tale of the Mariposas' fight to restore democracy. At the morgue, she snipped Maria Teresa's long braid of hair: it's one of the many venerable objects on display at the Mirabal family home in Conuco, where visitors can see items from the sisters' day-to-day lives. Also on display are objects from the day of the sisters' assassination, including the shoes they were wearing and the handbags they carried. Exactly four decades after their murder, the sisters' remains were moved to a burial site on the museum grounds.

📍 The museum is a short drive east of the town of Salcedo.

José Maria Sert Plaza

CLARA CAMPOAMOR

San Sebastián, Spain

Elected to Spain's Constituent Convention in 1931 despite the fact that women could not yet vote, Clara Campoamor grew up working class and at a young age took employment as a seamstress before going on to a career of advocating for women's rights. At the time, even the leftist party she belonged to opposed women's suffrage; but, through a passionate debate in front of the assembly, Campoamor convinced a majority to vote in favour of enshrining the women's vote within Spain's new constitution. Exiled from Spain during Franco's regime, Campoamor never backed down from her beliefs. Sculptures in her honour adorn cities from Madrid to Seville.

➡ Also in San Sebastián, her one-time home, Polloe Cemetery contains Campoamor's repatriated ashes.

© Roman Belogorodov / Alamy Stock Photo

© David Havel / Shutterstock

Karanambu Ranch

DIANE McTURK

North Rupununi, Guyana

Born in Guyana and educated in London, Diane McTurk (1932-2016) took her historic family cattle ranch in Guyana's savannah and in the 1970s turned it into a groundbreaking centre for giant river otter conservation and ecotourism. Her work inspired others in the region to follow suit, and nowadays the area abounds with environmentally oriented businesses. But it was McTurk's playful, kind and intensely charming personality, which so perfectly jibed with her otter 'kids' in the Rupununi River, that made her so beloved to her community and all who met her. Never afraid of being herself and following her heart, she worked on conservation efforts up to her death.

⬅ Bring binoculars. Besides river otters (pictured left), there are over 600 bird species to see around the ranch.

Ivy Green

HELEN KELLER

Tuscumbia, USA

If you learned about Helen Keller (1880-1968) in grade school, you probably remember the story of the well-pump. Keller, who'd become blind and deaf after an illness in toddlerhood, was sitting by the pump with her new teacher, Anne Sullivan. Sullivan had been trying to teach Keller fingerspelling, tracing letters on her palm. But 6-year-old Keller wasn't getting the connection between the sensations on her hand and what they were meant to represent. That day, Sullivan turned on the pump and ran Keller's hand under the water while spelling W-A-T-E-R in her other palm.

'I knew then that w-a-t-e-r meant the wonderful cool something that was flowing over my hand', Keller would write in her autobiography. Keller would go on to graduate from Radcliffe College and travel the world as a celebrated speaker and disability rights advocate. A dedicated socialist, she would fight for progressive causes from pacifism to birth control to women's rights, helping to found the American Civil Liberties Union in 1920. Sullivan would be her lifelong companion.

See the well-pump that opened up Keller's world at Ivy Green, her white clapboard childhood home. In late June, the house is the busy site of the Helen Keller Festival. In summer, *The Miracle Worker*, the play depicting her life with Sullivan, is performed on the Ivy Green grounds.

Ivy Green is in Tuscumbia, Alabama, about midway between Birmingham and Nashville.

Chinese Historical Society of America

MARY TAPE

San Francisco, USA

Mary Tape immigrated to the US in 1868, marrying and starting a family in San Francisco. She later fought to desegregate California schools in the landmark Tape v Hurley case of 1885, which she brought on behalf of her young daughter. The ruling won Chinese Americans the right to enrol in public schools in the state. Picture what it was like for Tape to be Chinese in America during the gold rush and transcontinental railroad construction eras in this museum. Exhibits share insights on Chinese American history, including the Chinese Exclusion Act, which barred Chinese immigrants from US citizenship from 1882 to 1943.

⬅ The Chinese Historical Society is housed in a 1932 landmark building, originally built as Chinatown's YWCA.

Place de la Concorde

OLYMPE DE GOUGES

Paris, France

French writer and political activist Olympe de Gouges (1748–1793) wrote plays and essays pressing for social change, especially concerning women's and children's rights and abolitionism. She lived during the French Revolution, and her radical 1791 pamphlet *Declaration of the Rights of Woman and the Female Citizen* called for parity between the genders. Olympe de Gouges called for civil disobedience to unjust laws – a stance common to later philosophers and advocates such as Thoreau, Gandhi and Martin Luther King, Jr. She was rewarded for her free-thinking by being executed at the guillotine in Place de la Concorde during the French Revolution's Reign of Terror.

➡ Marie Antoinette was also executed on this spot; back then it had been renamed the Place de la Révolution.

Rosa Luxemburg Memorial

ROSA LUXEMBURG

Berlin, Germany

'Freedom is always and exclusively freedom for the one who thinks differently.'

Noises from the nearby Berlin Zoo mix with the wheezes of passing joggers as you approach this slanted steel-and-bronze memorial. Spelling out R-O-S-A L-U-X-E-M-B-U-R-G in raised capital letters, it practically seems to slide into the murky Landwehr Canal. This is where visitors come to pay their respects every 15 January in homage to this sharp-minded and outspoken anti-war activist who is a key figure of revolutionary socialism.

On this wintry day in 1919, Luxemburg was shot by German paramilitary troops, her body dumped unceremoniously into the canal right on this spot. Her bold attempt to found a socialist republic on the heels of the German monarchy's failure had been cruelly cut short. The state-sanctioned murder put a brutal end to the brief, brave life of this tireless champion of the working class. Her rise to prominence in the male-dominated world of politics of her time continues to be an inspiration to radicals, freethinkers and activists today. Luxemburg's flame may have been snuffed, but her dream lives on.

♥ Just off the Landwehr canal is Berlin's zoo, holding a triple record as Germany's oldest (since 1844), most species-rich and most popular.

© Lee Thomas / Alamy Stock Photo

César E Chávez National Monument

DOLORES HUERTA

Bakersfield, USA

One of the most influential civil rights and labour activists of the 20th century, Dolores Huerta was the co-founder of the United Farm Workers Association with César Chávez. Originally a teacher, she began her career as an activist by lobbying politicians to allow non-US citizen migrant workers to receive public aid; holding voter registration drives among the workers; and fighting to provide Spanish-language driver's tests and voting ballots. She and Chávez, along with Gilbert Padilla, organised the now-famous 1965 national grape boycott in Delano. Chávez, a vibrant leader, and Huerta, a tough negotiator, catalysed all of the over 5000 farm workers to strike, and Huerta handled contract discussions. The continued boycotts of table grapes in the late 1960s led to a historic agreement between the workers and 26 grape growers, greatly improving working conditions for the farm workers. Victories included giving workers healthcare and unemployment benefits and reducing the use of poisonous pesticides.

Huerta later coordinated a national lettuce boycott in the 1970s and another boycott of grapes in 1973. Her work helped pave the way for passage of the 1975 Agricultural Labor Relations Act, the first law recognising farm workers' rights to form unions and bargain collectively. Huerta now leads her own foundation, organising communities to pursue social justice. Near the agricultural corridor of California's central valley, the César E Chávez National Monument honouring Huerta's comrade provides a concise overview of their work in the US labour movement.

 Visiting Northern California? Huerta was inducted into the California Museum's state Hall of Fame in 2013. It can be toured in Sacramento.

The Cathedral of Christ the Saviour

PUSSY RIOT

Moscow, Russia

Founded in August 2011, the feminist protest punk rock band Pussy Riot shot to prominence after their protest appearance at Moscow's Cathedral of Christ the Saviour on 21 February 2012, when the group serenaded those in attendance with their 'punk prayer'. Clad in balaclavas, Nadezhda Tolokonnikova, Maria Alyokhina, Yekatertina Samutsevich and two other bandmates used their lyrics to implore the Virgin Mother to 'deliver us from Putin' and made explicit reference to the alleged collaboration between Russian Orthodox priests and the KGB since the fall of Communism. Pussy Riot's choice of this Kremlin-adjacent cathedral as their protest venue was a guerrilla move criticised by some as 'blasphemous', and the protest galvanised both sides. Three members of Pussy Riot were sentenced to time in prison for the disruption, with two of them, young mothers, deliberately incarcerated far from their families.

Today the members of Pussy Riot continue to speak out at home and abroad, even invading the pitch at the 2018 World Cup final to stage a protest against Russian human rights abuses. Although they continue to face persecution (one World Cup protest member was hospitalised afterwards with poisoning symptoms), their demands for greater political freedom haven't been silenced despite the repercussions.

The vast, golden-domed cathedral was rebuilt in 1997 and can be visited daily from 10am to 6pm.

ESTABLISHMENT OF ROBBEN ISLAND MUSEUM: Nelson Mandela at the launch of the Robben Island Museum in 1997. In the background are sketches of other South African anti-apartheid leaders: Govan Mbeki, Mandela, Steve Biko, Robert Sobukwe and Walter Sisulu.

"We are Namibians and not South Africans. We do not now, and will not in the future recognise your right to govern us; to make laws for us in which we had no say; to treat our country as if it were your property and as if you were our masters. We have always regarded South Africa as an intruder in our country."

Statement by Andimba Toivo ja Toivo, a founder member of SWAPO, after he was sentenced to 20 years' imprisonment under the Suppression of Communism Act by the Supreme court in Pretoria on 25 January 1968. He and 36 other Namibians were charged with having participated in a scheme aimed at seizing revolution and armed resistance against the government and administration of Namibia.

Robben Island Museum

WINNIE MANDELA

Cape Town, South Africa

Winnie Madikizela-Mandela married Nelson Mandela in 1958, and they had two daughters before he was arrested and imprisoned in Robben Island, a former leper colony, off Cape Town. For decades, Winnie, a social worker by profession, was in many ways her husband's microphone for South Africa's black nationalist movement. Every six months for nearly twenty years, Winnie went to extraordinary lengths to see him on Robben Island: she had to apply for a permit to travel, check in with the police, take a flight from Johannesburg to Cape Town and then catch the ferry.

Winnie described Robben Island as cold and brutal. For 18 years, she was told that she and Nelson were only allowed to discuss family and their children – nothing else. Usually, six officers monitored the Mandelas' conversation, and if they didn't understand what the couple was talking about, they interrupted them or ended the visit. According to prison laws, the Mandela children couldn't meet their father until they were 16 years old, and Winnie admitted that she gave up witnessing many of her daughters' milestones to fight for justice in South Africa. Today, Robben Island is a Unesco World Heritage Site, and the prison has been transformed into a museum. Although the couple later divorced and Winnie forged her own (sometimes contentious) path, her strength and outspokenness during his imprisonment helped keep the anti-apartheid fight going, and the same grit powered her later career as a member of parliament in her own right.

The Robben Island Museum (shown above) is accessible by ferry from the Nelson Mandela Gateway at Cape Town's V&A Waterfront.

Workhouse Arts Center

LUCY BURNS

Lorton, USA

One American woman has the distinction of having spent more time in prison than any other suffragist. That woman is the total badass feminist hero Lucy Burns (1879–1966). The Lucy Burns Museum at the Occoquan Workhouse tells her story. Here is where Burns and her fellow suffragists endured the 'Night of Terror'. The women were brutally beaten and thrown into cells. Burns was made an example of and was hand-cuffed to a crossbar of her cell high above her head for the night in freezing conditions wearing nothing but a slip. Lucy Burns reminds us that to say American women were 'given' the right to vote in 1920 is just plain wrong: activists like her fought and fought hard to gain suffrage against the odds.

➡ Virginia's Workhouse Arts Center, just south of Washington, DC, is both artist studios and monument to penal history.

Savitribai Phule Pune University

SAVITRIBAI PHULE

Pune, India

Savitribai Phule was an intersectional feminist way before the term existed. Phule, together with her close Muslim friend, Fatime Begum Sheikh, started a school for India's lowest caste communities in 1849. She and her husband Jyotiba Phule (whom she married at the age of 9) also established a girls' school in Bhidewada in 1848. She was India's first female teacher, railing against child marriage and oppressive caste rituals. In a final swoop of achievement, she opened a clinic for those suffering from the bubonic plague; the act of mercy led to her own demise, yet you suspect she wouldn't do it differently.

⬅ In 2014 Pune University (left) was renamed in honour of Phule.

Shangla Village School

MALALA YOUSAFZAI

Swat Valley, Pakistan

Activist, author, and youngest-yet winner of the
Nobel Peace Prize (at 17), Malala Yousafzai didn't
survive a Taliban assassination attempt only to
rest on her laurels. After relocating to Birmingham
for medical treatment following an attack on her
school bus, she only intensified her outspokenness
around ensuring girls have fair access to
education, and she followed through on her
own educational commitment by enrolling at the
University of Oxford. Her Malala Fund raises money
for girls' education, and in 2018 even opened a
new school for girls in Shangla village near Malala's
childhood home in Pakistan's Swat Valley, though
she could only visit under the protection of an
armed guard. Yet with over 30 million girls around
the world still lacking an opportunity to receive
even a primary school education according to
Unicef, every new school counts. Malala herself
is proof of her memorable quote, 'One child, one
teacher, one book, one pen can change the world'.

📍 Birmingham's Centenary Square is a rather safer destination for
Malala fans looking to connect to her legacy.

© Shahid Khan / Alamy Stock Photo

©Joe Benning / Shutterstock

Women's Rights National Historical Park

ELIZABETH CADY STANTON

Seneca Falls, USA

'We hold these truths to be self evident; that all men and women are created equal.'

The Seneca Falls Convention fired forth its Declaration of Independence update in 1848 thanks in large part to the efforts of Elizabeth Cady Stanton (1815-1902), who split her time raising seven kids in upstate New York and championing women's rights across the country. Unlike most women's rights advocates, convention attendee Stanton wanted it all – not just the right to vote, but the right for divorce, sexual rights in marriage, right to property. Sometimes she was even seen as too radical by peers; her *Women's Bible* in the

1890s, calling out inherent sexism in religious doctrines, alienated many fellow suffragettes. She died 18 years before women got the vote in 1920, having lost much of the credit for her decades of work. Her lifelong collaborator Susan B Anthony always gave it back. Anthony would say this was her life's greatest happiness: 'When [Stanton] forged the thunderbolts and I fired them'.

While in Seneca Falls, be sure to also visit the National Women's Hall of Fame.

'Education should not mold the mind according to a prefabricated architectural plan. It should rather liberate the mind.'

Royce Hall, UCLA

ANGELA DAVIS

Los Angeles, USA

Now a professor emerita, activist Angela Davis first began her teaching career at UCLA, where her communist affiliation led the state regents to try firing Davis before her first lecture. Their effort backfired, and a rush of support led to Professor Davis giving her lectures in the 2000-person-capacity Royce Hall...until with Ronald Reagan's support, the regents successfully fired Davis later in the school year. Next, Davis turned her efforts to the fight on behalf of George Jackson, Fleeta Drumgo, and John Clutchette, three African American inmates known as the 'Soledad Brothers', who were accused of murdering a white prison guard. Although not herself present for the hostage takeover of a Marin County Courthouse involving the Soledad Brothers, Angela Davis was accused of aggravated kidnapping and first-degree murder. While underground, Davis was placed on the FBI's Ten Most Wanted Fugitive List. Upon capture, Davis faced the death penalty. People of all colours and creeds organised in support of Davis' release from prison. Forty years later Davis returned to Royce Hall as a Regents' Lecturer in 2014, showing how far her work has moved the political needle.

📍 Historic Royce Hall today hosts concerts as well as lectures.

Riksdagshuset
GRETA THUNBERG
Stockholm, Sweden

When she is not giving speeches around Europe on the urgency of tackling climate change right now, 16-year-old Greta Thunberg sits outside Stockholm's Parliament House (Riksdagshuset) every Friday with a placard, and intends to continue to do so until her government's policies are in line with the Paris climate agreement. It's hard to think of anyone more relevant today than Thunberg, a painfully shy girl with Asperger's, who first sat outside the Riksdagshuset in August 2018, and was eventually joined by more and more people. She's become an inspiration, speaking at Extinction Rebellion climate protests, and in March 2019, 1.4 million young people heeded her Climate Strike call to skip school and protest for more action on climate change.

The tireless Thunberg has been nominated for a Nobel Peace Prize and has shamed politicians in various countries, including the UN, for not taking timely action. She is a vegan, she travels by rail (and boat) instead of flying, and in 2019 she sailed across the Atlantic in a yacht to attend the UN Summit on Climate Change and then spent nine months giving talks around the Americas.

📍 Those inspired by Greta's example can take a #flyingless pledge or look up their local Extinction Rebellion chapter.

© Grisha Bruev / Shutterstock

White Rose Memorial
SOPHIE SCHOLL
Munich, Germany

On a quiet square outside of Munich's Ludwig Maximilian University, a pile of pamphlets made of bronze cover the cobblestone. This is the White Rose memorial, a tribute to student Sophie Scholl and her brother Hans, executed for their anti-Nazi protests during WWII. The White Rose was a secret activist group dedicated to nonviolence. Founders Sophie and Hans took to the streets of Munich and evaded SS patrols to distribute leaflets urging Germans to participate in passive resistance.

On 18 February 1943, White Rose activism caught up with its members. Sophie and Hans were arrested by the Nazis while giving out pamphlets at the university, found guilty of treason and beheaded by guillotine days later. Seeing the Gestapo approaching, Sophie is said to have thrown her remaining papers in the air. That moment is immortalised by the bronze replicas strewn on the ground. There are several streets, buildings and monuments dedicated to the Scholls throughout Germany, all reminders for the modern era that Sophie proved how even in oppressive and unjust times, there is no such thing as a small, insignificant act of defiance.

📍 The White Rose Memorial is located in Scholl Siblings Square, a short walk via Ludwigstrasse from the Universität station.

© anahtiris / Shutterstock, artist sculpture © Robert Schmidt-Matt

Race Street Meeting House

LUCRETIA MOTT

Philadelphia, USA

The unassuming yet stately Federal-style red-brick Race Street Meeting House, built in 1856, quickly became one of the most vital centres of abolitionism and women's suffrage in Philadelphia. Central to its efforts was the work of Quaker Lucretia Mott, whose outspoken defence of women's rights as well as the rights of African Americans made her one of the moral leaders of the Seneca Falls Convention. The meeting house's legacy continued into the 20th century with Quaker support of groups including Action AIDS.

← The meeting house has remained continuously active since opening; it's now a National Historic Landmark.

Cherokee National History Museum

WILMA MANKILLER

Tahlequah, USA

Wilma Mankiller (1945–2010) was born and bred an activist, from her youth in Oklahoma to her role as the first female principal chief of the second largest tribe in the United States: the Cherokee Nation. During her time as chief, from 1985 to 1995, she focused on social improvements through education, healthcare and job training. Until her death she was a champion of women's and Native American rights. Today, visitors to Cherokee Nation in Oklahoma can explore the history of the tribe she fought for tirelessly.

➡ Visit Cherokee Nation in Tahlequah, Oklahoma, for classes, events and exhibits.

© Jan Zeman / 500px

Wallenstein Palace

FRANTIŠKA PLAMÍNKOVÁ

Prague, Czech Republic

Czech feminist and suffrage activist Františka Plamínková began her career advocating that teachers have the right to marry. Later her career took her into journalism and into a Senate chair seat in the National Assembly. Connected to many international suffrage organisations and a strong civil liberties advocate, she was executed by the Gestapo in 1942. Today Františka is memorialised by a plaque within the beautiful gardens of Wallenstein Palace, seat of the Czech Senate.

← This huge, baroque garden is an oasis of peace amid the bustle of central Prague's streets.

White House of the Confederacy

MARY RICHARDS BOWSER

Richmond, USA

The remarkable Mary Richards Bowser (circa 1846–1867) was born into slavery in Virginia. Amazingly, after being freed, she joined a spy ring during the American Civil War. She went undercover, spying in the Confederate White House by posing as a slave. Not only that: the spy circle that she was a part of was run by Elizabeth Van Lew, part of the family who previously owned her. Throughout her life Richards Bowser used various pseudonyms, everything from Richmonia St Pierre to simply Mary Richards. She later became a teacher of emancipated African Americans.

→ The Confederate White House that Mary Richards Bowser infiltrated was located in Richmond, Virginia, and is operated as a museum now.

© Roger Viollet Collection / Getty Images

Kilmainham Gaol

COUNTESS MARKIEVICZ

Dublin, Ireland

'I am pledged as a rebel, an unconvertible rebel, to the one thing - a free and independent Republic.'

The 1916 Easter Rising leaders were all visitors in this hulking prison, and it was their executions here that most deeply etched the jail's name into Irish consciousness. Countess Constance Markievicz was held alongside these martyrs in a cell marked with her name which can still be visited today. The countess led a feature film-worthy life. She married a wealthy Polish-Ukrainian count and eventually moved to Dublin, where she became a firm believer in Ireland's Independence. Ten years later, the count moved back to Ukraine, leaving the countess to go about the business of liberating her country, which she did with revolutionary zeal. Like 14 other Easter Rising leaders, she was sentenced to death. But the execution of James Connolly, so badly injured that he had to be tied to a chair instead of standing in front of the firing squad, was a major tipping point. Authorities knew it would not look good to execute a woman — much less a rich one — and the countess was set free. The uprising failed in its immediate goals, but the tide had turned: Ireland would be free eventually. As for the countess, in 1918 she became the first woman to be elected to the UK's House of Commons (a seat she chose not to take due to her commitment to republicanism).

Kilmainham Gaol is on the southwest side of Dublin. It's an easy walk from Heuston Station.

Top 10 BLUE PLAQUES

Visitors to London may notice distinctive blue plaques on buildings across the city, marking sites linked to notable figures. Mostly maintained by the English Heritage Trust, they can also be found outside London thanks to local councils. Keep your eyes peeled for amazing women from all walks of life on these striking markers.

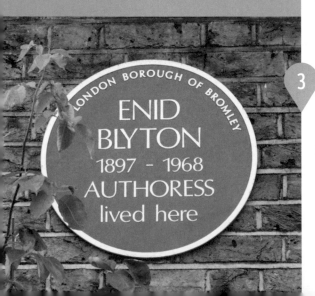

 ### 1 EMMELINE PANKHURST & DAME CHRISTABEL PANKHURST

50 Clarendon Rd, Notting Hill, London

Emmeline went to her first women's suffrage meeting at 14 years old, and her daughter Christabel was born into the movement. Emmeline founded the Women's Social and Political Union, who took a militant 'deeds not words stance'. Clarendon Rd was their base when women won a limited vote in 1918.

 ### 2 HANNAH BILLIG

198 Cable Street, East London

'Angel of Cable Street' Hannah Billig became a doctor in 1925, serving the East End for years, with an interlude in charge of Wapping's air raid shelters during the Blitz. Her service won her a George Medal, and a 1942 stint as a doctor with the Indian Army earned her an MBE.

 ### 3 ENID BLYTON

83 Shortlands Road, Bromley

Bestselling children's author Enid Blyton is beloved for her *Noddy, Famous Five* and *Secret Seven* books, to name just a few from this productive author. Over fifty years after her death, she remains the fourth most-widely translated writer ever.

 ### 4 SYLVIA PANKHURST

120 Cheyne Walk, Chelsea, London

Emmeline Pankhurst's other activist daughter lived in this blue Chelsea home from 1906 to 1909, a period which saw her arrested for protests in favour of women's suffrage. Sylvia later founded the leftist East London Federation of Suffragettes, and she fought fiercely against WWI and, later, fascism.

 ### 5 MARY SEACOLE

14 Soho Square, Soho, London

Jamaican-born Mary Seacole left the Caribbean for England intending to join the nursing ranks of the Crimean War. Rejected due to her colour, she went to the Crimea to tend to the wounded anyway and published her autobiography after.

6 FANNY BURNEY

11 Bolton Street, Mayfair, London

The first blue plaque to a woman was erected for Fanny Burney, part of Samuel Johnson's circle and the orbit of the Bluestockings. Virginia Woolf called her 'the mother of English fiction' for her influence on the next generation of authors through works such as *Camilla*.

7 ELIZABETH GOULD BELL

Daisyhill Hospital, Newry, Northern Ireland

Dr Bell was one of the first women to qualify as a doctor in Ireland. An active suffragette herself, during Belfast's suffragette hunger strike Dr. Bell gave medical care to the imprisoned women undergoing force feedings in jail.

8 HERTHA AYRTON

41 Norfolk Sq, Paddington, London

The first woman admitted into the Institution of Electrical Engineers (in 1899 – the next to join would be in 1958!), Hertha Ayrton studied maths at Cambridge and was awarded the Royal Society's Hughes Medal (but denied membership). At 41 Norfolk Sq she developed the Ayrton fan, used in WWI to dispel poison gases.

9 JOANNA BAILLIE

Bolton House, Windmill Hill, Hampstead

Scottish dramatist and poet Baillie received the fourth plaque (brown rather than blue) dedicated to a woman at the Hampstead home where she lived for 50 years. Lord Byron, Sir Walter Scott, Keats and Wordsworth all visited her here.

10 JESSICA ACE & MARGARET WRIGHT

Mumbles Pier, Swansea, Wales

When the ship *Admiral Prinz Adalbert* ran into a fierce 1883 storm here and the Mumbles lifeboat was endangered, Jessica Ace and Margaret Wright sprang into action, saving crew with their heroism. They were not officially thanked at the time by the Royal National Lifeboat Institution.

ARTISTS

Casa Azul

FRIDA KAHLO

Mexico City, Mexico

Hands down the most internationally recognisable female artist, Frida Kahlo (1907–1954) was born in this beautiful blue house in Mexico City's leafy Coyoacán district. She spent much of her life here, some with husband and prominent muralist Diego Rivera, and died here as well. Kahlo's childhood home, now a museum, is the most complete homage to her memory there is. It is obvious why she cherished Casa Azul, which enchantingly encloses a courtyard and garden. And a tour reveals why she became such a celebrated painter, with walls decorated by many of her finest works.

Kahlo employed the much-loved folk art style to break new ground in a machismo-dominated artistic world, exploring gender, race and class. Themes in her work included chronic pain and her spinal injury, sustained in an accident at age 18. Despite her entering into a tempestuous marriage with the then better-known Rivera, her work soon attracted international attention. The Louvre even made a Kahlo painting the first they acquired from a Mexican artist. And her art world standing snowballed posthumously: the word 'Fridamania' came to describe the phenomenon. A reconsidering of art history from new perspectives saw her take her place as one of Mexico's all-time greatest artists and cultural exports. Utterly compelling Casa Azul shows her gifts in context with her fascinating life.

📍 Museo Dolores Olmedo, in the Xochimilco neighbourhood, also has a room reserved for Frida Kahlo's paintings.

Maison George Sand

GEORGE SAND

Nohant-Vict, France

Strolling the manicured, flower-rimmed grounds and orchards of the 18th-century manor estate where French Romantic novelist George Sand (1804-1876) spent much of her life, you might assume she led a charmed existence. The truth is far more unconventional, but the writer did have a profound love for this haven in central France.

Born Amantine Lucile Aurore Dupin in Paris, she was raised by her paternal grandmother at this estate, which often glowed with the creativity of illustrious society: Flaubert, Balzac, Liszt and Delacroix, and most famously Chopin – the composer-pianist who spent seven summers here and with whom she became embroiled in a long, stormy affair. One of many, in fact.

Today, gilt-framed portraits of the writer hang on flock-papered walls in her one-time home's gracious parlours, many depicting a raven-haired beauty with a mysterious look in her eye. Yet while many women of her class fussed over corsets, she was busy subverting the bourgeois stereotype of the proper lady. Going by her *nom de plume* George Sand, the author forged an androgynous, cross-dressing identity, and even brazenly smoked in public. She was politically active, writing for the *Figaro* newspaper and acting as minister for propaganda after the 1848 Revolution. And she was the most successful French author of her age, more so even than Victor Hugo, who sung Sand's praises in his obituary in her honour.

Nohant-Vic is in the Berry province of central France, around an hour's drive south of the city of Bourges.

'Tell the truth, but tell it slant.'

Emily Dickinson Museum

EMILY DICKINSON

Amherst, USA

The Emily Dickinson Museum is a monument to the girl who practically invented emo. No one knows for sure what kept the 'Belle of Amherst' inside her home for most of her adult life – modern scholars have guessed everything from agoraphobia or epilepsy as the cause – but her reclusive ways certainly helped build her brand. Emily didn't get out much, but rumours about her sure did. She only wore white, they said. She would talk to guests to her home through a crack in her bedroom door. She was obsessed with death. In reality Emily Dickinson was a much more relatable figure. Death and mortality were common themes of her poetry, but they were equally common themes in contemporary society. Dickinson's unique poems forged from these topics, the bulk of which she composed on a tiny desk in her bedroom, are sui generis. Visitors to the museum can see that little desk, which she equated with freedom. As well as her desk, see the poet's bed and the basket she would lower out her window to send the neighbourhood children treats.

Amherst is ideally situated just under two hours from Boston. It's the perfect midway point when taking your bookish daughter around to visit liberal arts colleges in the East.

'Without the energy that lifts mountains, how am I to live?'

Meera Temple

MEERABAI

Chittorgarh, India

Meerabai (1498-1546), mystic, saint and poetess, also has the (reputed) distinction of having survived attempted assassination by poison. A princess herself, she married into an aristocratic family and prepared to settle into domesticity. But then her husband died in the region's Rajput–Mughal wars, and everything in her life changed.

Born at the dawn of the 16th century, Meerabai's life as a widow had already been scripted for her: the unconscionable tradition of following her husband into his funeral pyre, or living out her life in quiet penitence. She did neither, choosing instead to devote her life to Lord Krishna, holding *satsangs* (spiritual discourses) and writing *bhajans* (hymns) in praise of him. Her family was outraged at her aberrant behaviour. Others made attempts on her life. Miraculously, she survived them all, becoming an ambulatory saint. 'Nobody can prevent me from going to the saints. I don't care what the people say,' she sang, expressing the sentiments of Hinduism's Bhakti movement.

Cocooned within her small jewel-box of a sanctuary, the intricately etched stone temple devoted to Krishna, she spent her days singing Lord Krishna's praise. Today, you'll find a beautiful white statue in her stead at the temple, seated forever next to her beloved Krishna. It's the ideal place to peruse a volume of her poetry.

📍 The Meerabai temple sits inside a much larger Vishnu temple complex. It is about a three-hour drive from Jodhpur, and an hour away from Pushkar.

Sissinghurst Castle Garden

VITA SACKVILLE-WEST

Kent, England

Poet and novelist Vita Sackville-West (1892–1962) was a member of the infamous Bloomsbury Set and a friend of Virginia Woolf, but is perhaps better known for her garden at Sissinghurst Castle. Over 30 years, she transformed the garden into one of England's most loved. She designed an experimental, informal planting scheme on the grounds that flows through a series of themed outdoor garden rooms, such as the White Garden, the Rose Garden, the Lime Walk and the Cottage Garden. Although neither a trained horticulturalist nor a designer, her planting schemes remain some of the most influential of all time.

National Library of Antigua and Barbuda

JAMAICA KINCAID

St John's, Antigua and Barbuda

Author Jamaica Kincaid chronicled the history of Antigua and Barbuda's National Library starting with her childhood infatuation with the books here and the earthquake of 1974 that destroyed it, decrying its paltry replacement above a dry goods store. It took the post-colonial government decades before they prioritised a replacement, finally opening a new library on Market Street next to Victoria Park. Now a Professor of African and African American Studies in Residence at Harvard University, Kincaid's *Lucy* among other works reflect on her experiences growing up in St John's before leaving to work in the states at age 16.

📍 Take the train to Staplehurst or Arriva 5 bus service from Maidstone. The site is now operated by the National Trust.

📍 Visit the library en route to Coconut Grove, arguably the best beach bar on the island.

Museo Gabriela Mistral

GABRIELA MISTRAL

Vicuña, Chile

Lucila Godoy Alcayaga, who went by the pen name Gabriela Mistral, is best known as the first Latin American writer to win the Nobel Prize in Literature. A gifted poet, educator, and diplomat, she also served as Chilean consul in Italy, Spain and Portugal. But before all of the international recognition, Mistral was a humble schoolteacher from a poor family in the Andean village of Montegrande, Chile: her childhood home, now a museum, shows the simplicity of her early life. While supporting her seamstress mother with her income from the elementary school, Mistral wrote poems on the side, and life handed her a fair share of joys and disappointments to explore in her work. A pair of heartbreaks inspired Mistral's first notable works, *Sonetos de la muerte* (Sonnets on Death) in 1914 and *Desolación* (Despair) in 1922. She went on to write about romantic love, family relationships, grief, religion, and morality in the years that followed, travelling all over the world in her roles as a poet and diplomat. After her 1957 death in Hempstead, New York, her remains were returned to Chile, and the country observed three days of national mourning.

📍 The museum is located in the small town of Montegrande, easily accessible by bus from the city of La Serena

© TimAbbott / Getty Images

'Thank goodness I was never sent to school; it would have rubbed off some of the originality.'

Hill Top
BEATRIX POTTER
Cumbria, England

Beatrix Potter's beautifully illustrated tales flowed from her nib and paintbrush one after the next when she moved to Hill Top farm in Cumbria's Lake District in 1905. Nearly forty at the time, she used the royalties from *The Tale of Peter Rabbit* to purchase the farm, moved out of London and wholeheartedly embraced rural life in the countryside she had come to love during annual holidays. Close to the shores of mountain-rimmed Lake Windermere, the idyllic 17th-century farm in roughcast stone was both the inspiration and the backdrop for many of her most famous tales, and avid fans will be able to spy many familiar scenes. The rambling cottage garden, overgrown with foxgloves, lupins, roses and honeysuckle in summer, recalls *The Tale of Tom Kitten,* not to mention the rhubarb patch where Jemima Puddle-Duck hid her eggs. Beatrix oversaw the design of the garden herself, then set about illustrating it in minute detail. The house is crammed with ink drawings, watercolours, letters, ceramics, antique furniture and clothing including the author's hat and clogs. It's as if it has fallen into a fairytale-like slumber; Potter decreed her home be left for visitors 'as if I had just gone out and they had just missed me', and so it remains.

Besides being a prolific author and illustrator, Beatrix fiercely campaigned on local conservation issues. A Lake District landowner, farm manager and businesswoman, she actively championed the value of women in rural communities.

 You can reach Hill Top most fancifully by taking the ferry from Bowness to the west shore of Windermere.

© pxl.store / Shutterstock

Mbuantua Gallery

EMILY KAME KNGWARREYE

Alice Springs, Australia

Emily Kame Kngwarreye (1910–96), one of Australia's most important artists, was an Anmatyerre woman who lived and worked in Utopia, 230km (143 mi) northeast of Alice Springs. Despite being one of the most successful artists in Australia's history (her paintings have sold for up to A\$2.1 million), she didn't take up painting seriously until she was nearly 80 years old.

Kngwarreye's work draws on her deep connection to her country, Alhalkere, and her paintings interpret the 50,000+ years' uninterrupted heritage of her ancestors living there. She encodes the Dreaming, the landscape, clan knowledge, seasons and ancestral designs in her work, gained through decades spent in close observation and relationship with her country. Like other artists from the amazing arts communities of the Central Desert, she painted many of her canvases sitting cross-legged on the ground in the open air, the red soil of her country beneath the canvas. Kngwarreye painted around 3400 artworks in the seven years before her death and, in keeping with kinship obligations, she distributed her earnings within her community.

Her paintings are highly sought after in international collections, but you can purchase some of her smaller works (starting around \$35,000) through Mbantua Gallery in Alice Springs.

📍 Utopia, home to around 2000 aboriginal people, covers approximately 1 million square acres of land northeast of Alice Springs.

St Mary's on the Island Cemetery
LAURENCE HOPE
Chennai, India

In an overgrown cemetery lies the grave of the extraordinary poet Laurence Hope – aka 'Violet' Nicolson – who killed herself in Madras (now Chennai) in 1904.

'Mr' Hope's exotic, erotic, gender-bending poetry thrilled readers from London to New York. When 'he' was outed as the wife of a high-ranking British army officer in India, the ensuing scandal made her infamous. It was brief fame. Devastated by her husband's unexpected death, she killed herself aged 39. Now, beneath rampant post-monsoon vegetation, she lies, buried above him, in a single grave.

← Laurence Hope's grave is in the cemetery of St Mary's-on-the-Island in Chennai.

Westminster Abbey
APHRA BEHN
London, England

'All women together, ought to let flowers fall upon the grave of Aphra Behn...for it was she who earned them the right to speak their minds.' So said Virginia Woolf of this early female writer, a libertine and even spy in her day, best known for her final novel, *Oroonoko: or the Royal Slave*. Born of obscure origins around the year 1640, by the time of her death in 1689 Aphra Behn was the second most prolific English Reformation author after John Dryden, and the first known Englishwoman to make her living as a writer. King Charles II regularly attended her plays, and on her death, she was laid to rest in Westminster Abbey.

➡ Aphra Behn's life coincided with the English Restoration's theatrical resurgence. Plays of hers were produced at the Theatre Royal in Drury Lane, still standing.

'A woman must have money and a room of her own if she is to write fiction.'

Monk's House

VIRGINIA WOOLF

Rodmell, England

A veritable stream of arts world A-listers came calling at this bucolic, East Sussex village cottage, including Bloomsbury Group members TS Eliot, EM Forster, Vanessa Bell and Duncan Grant. And the reason they came was the cottage's owner, Virginia Woolf, one of the 20th century's greatest authors. Together with husband Leonard Woolf she purchased this writer's retreat in 1919 to escape London's freneticism, and the couple increasingly spent more time here up to her death. Monk's House consequently displays many insights into the Woolfs' colourful lives and associations: paintings by Bell and Grant, the glorious garden which was Leonard's creation and the shed at the bottom where Virginia produced much of her major writing.

Woolf fans will relish how her life and work come alive throughout. Oval tiling around Virginia's bedroom fireplace, for example, depicts a lighthouse that recalls *To the Lighthouse*. It was whilst waiting for this room to be completed that she wrote the feminist essay *A Room of One's Own*. Profits from *Mrs Dalloway* apparently paid for the bathroom, and Woolf's choice of colours still adorns many rooms.

But Monk's House is not just a marvellous collection of things by a couple with abundant talent and taste; it is a window into the life of the last century's most pivotal writers.

📍 Take bus 123 between Newhaven and Lewes to the nearby Abergavenny Arms in Rodmell, or cycle here on The Egrets Way.

Casa Madre

ALICE WALKER

Costa Careyes, Mexico

More than anyone I know, Alice Walker sees this earth as one Living Being — as in the title of her early poetry book, *Her Blue Body, Everything We Know*.

I always imagine her in places way more rural than urban, say, as a little girl finding a secret place to write under a tree in rural Georgia; in one of the many beautiful gardens her mother created on land her family could farm but not own; in the hills of Northern California where Alice has created her own home and cascade of gardens. Now, I imagine Alice where I have just seen her, on the coast of Mexico, in a house she created that nestles into a green acre of palm trees, natural stone sculptures, and running fountains.

Our mutual home country is going through a painful time, so it feels right that she is far enough away to see it clearly. Alice's world has no walls or borders, but migratory paths that cover the globe like lace.

BY GLORIA STEINEM

Top Withens

EMILY BRONTË

Keighley, England

At the nearby Brontë Parsonage Museum in Haworth, visitors can see the parlour where Emily died at the heartbreakingly young age of 30, just three months after her brother Branwell's death. But fans of the sole, brilliant creation of this middle Brontë sister, *Wuthering Heights*, candidate for most powerful and disturbing novel in the English language, can press on from the home to all the siblings and walk up to Top Withens. The ruined 17th-century house was said by a lifelong friend of Charlotte's to have inspired the brooding *Wuthering Heights* farmhouse. That makes it the scene of Cathy and Heathcliff's childhood, the haunting ice-cold hand through the casement that terrifies the pompous narrator, the brutal treatment of Isabella, and the blossoming love story of young Catherine and Hareton Earnshaw. Readers have struggled to connect the appearance of Top Withens with descriptions of the 'old and dark' house of the novel, but the setting is moody enough. Whether or not Top Withens was a direct inspiration for Emily, the walk there provides a wonderful immersion in the wild landscape that was the bedrock of her imagination. Listen out for lapwings and, in late summer and autumn, sniff the 'pure heather-scented air'.

📍 Top Withens can be reached on an 11 km (7 mile) circular walk from Haworth parsonage, passing the Brontë waterfall.

© Julie Mayfeng / Shutterstock

72 rue de Belleville
ÉDITH PIAF
Paris, France

Iconic French singer Édith Piaf (1915–1963) was brought up unconventionally in the rough Parisian suburb Belleville. As a child she joined her father touring Europe as a busker and then went out on her own. At 20 she was discovered, and 'The Little Sparrow' began her rise as a chanteuse. Piaf lived a tumultuous life, with multiple dalliances and marriages, plus two car wrecks that left her injured and addicted to alcohol and morphine. She poured her pain and passion into her music, with landmark songs like 'La Vie en Rose'. Her epic version of 'Non, Je Ne Regrette Rien' remains a staple. She is buried in Père Lachaise Cemetery next to her daughter, who died at the age of 2.

← Edith Piaf is said to have been born on the doorstep at 72 rue de Belleville in the 20th arrondissement; a plaque marks the spot.

Irma Stern Museum
IRMA STERN
Cape Town, South Africa

Irma Stern (1894-1966) was South Africa's very own Gauguin, a larger-than-life character who travelled to collect artefacts and inspiration for her expressive portraits and landscapes. With German Jewish heritage, she studied in Weimar and Berlin, associating with Max Pechstein and the German Expressionists, before returning to Cape Town and unleashing modernism on the conservative local art world. Her painterly style and depiction of black African women provoked outrage and she was investigated by the police for immorality. She persevered, and by 1927 she was living and painting in the Victorian pile that became a centre of bohemian life and now houses her museum.

→ The museum is 8km (5 mi) from the city centre via the M3 highway, near the main University of Cape Town campus.

Courtesy: Irma Stern Museum Trust Collection. Photo: Sean Wilson

Green Gables

LM MONTGOMERY

Prince Edward Island, Canada

Many a childhood fan of writer LM Montgomery (1874–1942) wished they could have snapped their fingers to be transported to a rambling farmhouse on Prince Edward Island, circa 1870 (with red hair, obviously).Does any bookish little girl not adore Anne of Green Gables? Her whirring imagination, her stout heart, her knees skinned from adventure. Introduced in 1908 in the eponymous book, she's been stealing hearts ever since, and drawing pilgrims to pay homage on the Prince Edward Island that was Anne's unforgettable setting, and where her creator, Lucy Maud Montgomery, was born. It remains one of the world's most glorious places to ramble, dreaming of Anne all the while – golden meadows, pebbled shores fringed with sea roses, creamy green farmland dotted with tranquil grazing cows.

 Green Gables, the farm that inspired Montgomery, is in the town of Cavendish, and open to visitors.

'You must get an education. You must go to school, and you must learn to protect yourself. And you must learn to protect yourself with the pen, and not the gun.'

Folies-Bergère
JOSEPHINE BAKER
Paris, France

When Josephine Baker (1906-1975) came on stage at the Folies-Bergère wearing little more than a skirt made of 16 rubber bananas, Paris lost its collective mind. It was 1926, and Baker's *danse sauvage* was like nothing anyone had ever seen. Her gyrations, all jerking pelvis and flying elbows, set to the beat of an African drum, fed Paris' fascination with 'exotic' black culture. Baker made the Belle Époque cabaret *the* place to be.

Baker had grown up not in a jungle but in raw poverty in St Louis. She propelled herself to international fame through fierce will. Today's most dramatic divas can't shake a peacock's feather at her extravagantly eccentric life – adopting a

'rainbow tribe' of 12 children from around the globe, outfitting her medieval French chateau with a mini golf course, frisking around town with a pet cheetah. All while she managed to be a French Resistance agent and Civil Rights icon.

When Baker hit the Folies-Bergère, the iconic cabaret was already more than 50 years old. It's still going strong today. Revel in its grandeur: imposing art deco façade, gilded turquoise lobby lined with tree-sized candelabras, twinkling red and gold music hall. You won't see any banana dances today, but you can catch modern musicals and rock acts. They may not be quite the spectacle that Baker was, but who ever will be?

📍 The Folies-Bergère still puts on shows at 32 rue Richer in Paris' 9th arrondissement.

'Never let go of that fiery sadness called desire.'

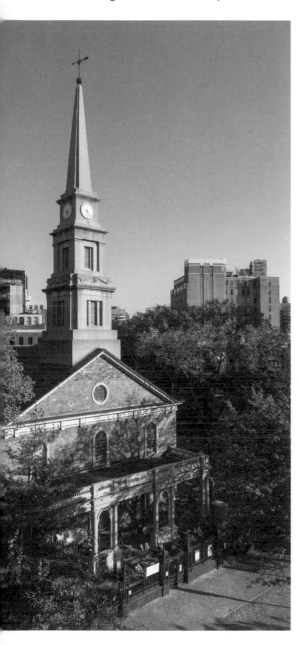

St Mark's Church-in-the-Bowery
PATTI SMITH
Manhattan, USA

It was 10 February 1971, a stingingly cold Wednesday night, and every scenester in Manhattan was at church. Andy Warhol was there. So were Lou Reed, and Sam Shepard, and Robert Mapplethorpe. They weren't at St Mark's Church in-the-Bowery to get their souls saved, but for something even more spiritual. Patti Smith was about to go on stage for the first time.

'My goal was not simply to do well, or hold my own', Smith later wrote. 'It was to make a mark at St. Mark's ... I wanted to infuse the written word with the immediacy and frontal attack of rock and roll'.

She did just that. Still several years from punk music stardom, the young poet was a vision in snakeskin boots, her friend Lenny Kaye accompanying with crashing guitar chords. After dedicating the evening to 'thieves', she read poems like 'Oath', which would later transform into the lyrics to her version of the song 'Gloria' ('Christ died for somebody's sins but not mine'). The crowd exploded. It's not what you'd expect to see in a house of worship, but St Mark's has never been an ordinary church. Built in the 1790s, the modest stone building has a long history of hosting avant-garde literature, dance and theatre. Check the online schedule to catch a reading or performance by the next Patti Smith.

St Mark's is at 131 E 10th Street in Manhattan's East Village.

Courtesy of Library of Congress

27 rue de Fleurus
GERTRUDE STEIN
Paris, France

American writer Gertrude Stein (1874–1946) was an iconic fixture in the Paris arts scene. She moved there in 1903 and was known not only for her modernist writing but for her famous salon, where she entertained other writers and artists like Ernest Hemingway, F Scott Fitzgerald and Ezra Pound. She was also an avid, early collector of the Cubists and Post-Impressionists like Pablo Picasso and Henri Matisse, giving their careers a boost. Picasso himself painted a famous portrait of Stein in 1905. Later, she would coin the term 'The Lost Generation' for the post-WWI writers in Paris in the 1920s. Stein lived for many years with her companion, Alice B Toklas, subject of Stein's major work *The Autobiography of Alice B Toklas*.

📍 Gertrude Stein's famous artistic salon was at 27 rue de Fleurus in Paris' 6th arrondissement on the Left Bank, and it is still marked by a plaque.

'Don't compromise yourself. It's all you've got.'

Hippie Hill
JANIS JOPLIN
San Francisco, USA

Stride across the grass on the eastern side of San Francisco's Golden Gate Park and you can almost hear the soulful strains of Janis Joplin. The legendary rock musician strummed her guitar beneath a tree here, in a section of the park dubbed 'Hippie Hill' in the '60s. The spot was a magnet for freethinkers, peace activists and long-haired youths looking to tune out. Today Hippie Hill is as likely to attract couples and picnickers, but impromptu musical performances still salute the spirit of Joplin, who died a legend aged only 27.

📍 The hill is a 15-minute walk west from 635 Ashbury St, where Joplin lived in the late '60s.

Osun Sacred Grove

SUSANNE WENGER

Osogbo, Nigeria

Nigeria's forests once protected numberless sacred sights, but urbanisation and deforestation have taken a sorry toll on these special places. One of the most important remaining groves is the Unesco-listed river and primary forest site of Osun, on the fringes of the wonderful art city of Osogbo. It's been protected thanks to the passionate efforts of Susanne Wenger, a surrealist Austrian artist who came to live in Nigeria in the 1950s. When she was cured of tuberculosis by a local herbalist, she embraced Yoruba beliefs, becoming a priestess who was granted the name Aduni Olosa, the 'Adored One'. A visit to Wenger's home in Osogbo, crammed with votive sculptures and ornate carved chairs, is unforgettable – and still very much a household shrine. But the grove itself is where you will see Wenger's towering artworks, created in collaboration with Nigerian artists. Yoruba people come here to worship fertility goddess Osun, especially during a processional festival held each summer. Monkeys scamper round the grove, snakes and antelope inhabit the forest, alligators lie in the sacred waters and 200 medicinal plants make the grove a vital resource. As well as this environmental and spiritual legacy, Wenger's influence lives on in the Osogbo's artist community, which is dotted with workshops and galleries.

📍 Wenger's adopted children, traditional priests Sangodare (0803 226 2188) and Doyin Faniyi (0803 226 2188) give excellent grove tours.

Casa das Histórias

PAULA REGO

Cascais, Portugal

In the pretty seaside town of Cascais, the last thing you expect to see are modern-day pyramids bearing the hallmark of Pritzker Prize-winning architect Eduardo Souto de Moura. But then visual artist Paula Rego has always liked to shock. So the pyramids sheltering the Casa das Histórias museum are a fitting backdrop for presenting the largest, most impressive body of her work.

It's all about the stories in her singular paintings, drawings and etchings – but not the kind you'd want to read as bedtime stories. These are nightmarish fairytales gone wrong, full of psychosexual intrigue as seen from a distinctly feminist viewpoint. Abuse, torture, murder, female suffering – it's all in the mix. The characters are grotesque and unsettling, their messages subversive. Rego's work doesn't make for easy viewing, and for a woman whose aim has been to 'give fear a human face', she presumably wouldn't have it any other way.

One of Portugal's most famous living artists, her career is as long as it is prolific, spanning more than 50 years. She began exhibiting as the only female artist with the London Group in the 1960s, alongside Lucian Freud and David Hockney, and became the first associate artist at the National Gallery in 1990. In 1998 she produced her controversial abortion etchings in response to Portugal's narrowly defeated referendum to legalise abortion, and in an attempt to encourage more women to vote for their rights in the future.

📍 The gallery is located in Cascais, a 40-minute train ride west of Cais do Sodré station in Lisbon.

Haida Gwaii

EMILY CARR

British Columbia, Canada

The islands of Haida Gwaii are the traditional lands of the Haida First Nation. In the early 1900s Emily Carr, an artist born in Victoria, BC, travelled solo to this remote archipelago, an extremely unusual venture for a woman of her time. Many of her paintings reflect the totem poles, hand-carved canoes, misty rainforests, and other elements of the Haida peoples' lives and landscapes. Carr remained relatively little-known until late in her life, but her paintings illustrating these First Nation communities have made her one of Canada's most important early 20th-century painters.

← Air Canada and Pacific Coastal Airlines fly from Vancouver. BC Ferries travel to the islands from Prince Rupert.

Kamala Surayya Memorial

KAMALA DAS

Thrissur, India

In her memoirs and confessional poems, both in English and Malayalam, Kamala Das railed against norms, social conventions, marital abuse and even tradition. She was frank in her writings on sexual love, lust and adultery. Her critics (mostly male) dismissed her talent as mere titillation. Her fans (mostly female) applauded her for an honest portrayal of the patriarchy, and in 1984 Das was nominated for the Nobel Prize in Literature. Fifteen years later she converted from Hinduism to Islam, taking the name Kamala Surayya. Today the Kamala Surayya Memorial, a rather dull-looking building that captures none of her vividness and vivacity, commemorates her work.

➡ Approximately two and a half hours from Kochi (in Kerala). Take a taxi to Punnayurkalam in Thrissur district.

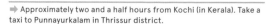

National Jazz Museum

BILLIE HOLIDAY

Harlem, USA

Billie Holiday (1915-1959) is widely considered one of the most influential jazz singers in history, thanks to her silky vocals, masterful command of cadence and unique stylistic delivery. She was born in Baltimore, Maryland, and grew up practising along to records of jazz greats including Louis Armstrong and Bessie Smith; her family moved to New York City in the late 1920s, and this transition would be instrumental in forming the foundation of Holiday's iconic music career. It was there in Harlem where Holiday began performing at nightclubs, and the rest is history. She went on to record such hits as 'What a Little Moonlight Can Do', 'Lover Man', 'I'll Be Seeing You', and the haunting 'Strange Fruit', which was named the 'song of the century' by *Time* magazine in 1999.

Holiday's work effectively defined the jazz genre, and there's no better place to learn about her legacy than the National Jazz Museum in Harlem. Not only does the museum have informative exhibitions, but it also hosts live music events – check their calendar before you make the pilgrimage to catch a show.

To really dive into the history of jazz in Harlem, take a tour of the Apollo, the emblematic venue that hosted some of the most important jazz acts to ever play, including Lady Day.

© Shanshan0312 / Shutterstock

'True originality consists not in a new manner but in a new vision.'

The Mount
EDITH WHARTON

Lenox, USA

Like her most memorable characters, Edith Wharton was raised in the airless realm of aristocratic Old New York. Born Edith Newbold Jones in 1862, she was schooled by private governesses, escorted on European tours and, at 17, 'presented' to society at a debutante ball. But clever little red-haired Edith was always an uneasy fit in this world (she was ditched by her first fiancé for 'an alleged preponderance of intellectuality'). Her eventual marriage, to Teddy Wharton, was the definition of 'good on paper'. But the Whartons were miserably incompatible, and Edith grew weary of the endless rounds of tennis parties and evenings at the opera. In 1901 she engineered an escape: building a property in the hills of Western Massachusetts. Edith Wharton would name the house The Mount, and she would blossom here.

She plunged into landscape architecture and gardening, and most importantly, she wrote. *The House of Mirth* and *Ethan Frome* were both written here (mostly in her bed). Today, visitors can wander the then-trendy enfiladed rooms decorated with the spoils of European holidays, roam the handsome gardens, and stay for readings and literary lectures. Edith's reverie here lasted only a decade – in 1912 Teddy sold the property for the equivalent of more than $4.5 million today. The pair divorced the following year, and Edith left America for Paris...and the rest of her life.

The Mount is in Lenox, Massachusetts, west of Boston in the Berkshires.

Staten Island's North Shore

AUDRE LORDE

Staten Island, USA

'I am deliberate and afraid of nothing.'

Although only a 25-minute ferry ride separates it from Manhattan, Staten Island feels a world away from the rest of New York City. It's easy to imagine this relative seclusion fuelling the mind of feminist writer Audre Lorde (1934-1992). The philosopher-poet wrote some of her most important works from her home at 207 St Paul's Ave. Lorde is credited with helping to articulate the principles underpinning intersectional feminist theory. While established patriarchal orders attempt to position women of colour and queer women as less worthy, Lorde called for these identities to be considered strengths – and she decried the failure of white feminists to uplift all women.

During her Staten Island years, from 1972 to 1987, Lorde founded Kitchen Table: Women of Color Press together with fellow feminist Barbara Smith. Feminist anthologies, and pamphlets leading the charge for activists of colour, rolled off the press.

The olive-green house in which Lorde lived can only be admired from outside. Still, the neighbourhood's atmosphere evokes what Lorde admired about Staten Island's balance of city and nature, backdrop to her revolutionary words.

📍 Arriving by ferry at the St George terminal, board bus S78 to St Paul's Ave/Paxton St to glimpse Lorde's house.

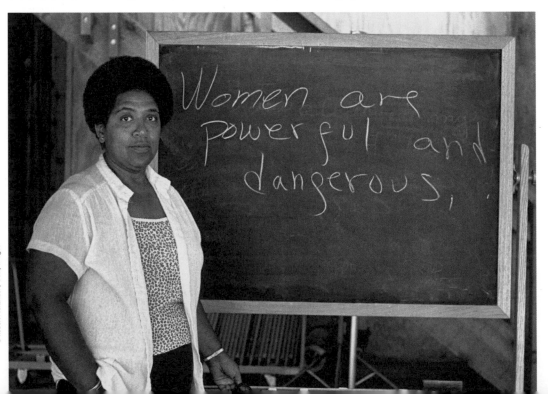

Pacific Crest Trail

CHERYL STRAYED

California—Washington, USA

It's hardcore hiking along the Pacific Crest Trail that runs from Mexico to Canada, but to do so alone, unprepared, suffering from grief and dealing with addiction makes it a spectacular feat of bravery bordering on crazy. Cheryl Strayed not only undertook this adventure but shared her experience with the world in heart-wrenching, unforgettable prose in her book *Wild: From Lost to Found on the Pacific Crest Trail* (later made into a movie by Reese Witherspoon). Anyone who has read *Wild* will forever equate the PCT with Strayed, and hikers on the spine of the Sierra Nevada and Cascade mountains can feel almost as if they are there with her, blisters and all.

Strayed has also extended her empathy and wisdom into the raw, straight-talking advice-column-turned-book *Dear Sugar*. Strayed's skill lies in taking her own life experiences, from growing up in a broken family and her mother's untimely death from cancer to her own divorce, and using them to expose universal truths. Aside from writing, Strayed has been an advocate in many feminist and progressive causes including VIDA: Women in Literary Arts, which works towards boosting traditionally marginalised voices of the writing community.

There are myriad trailheads in California, Oregon and Washington that access the Pacific Crest Trail.

Georgia O'Keeffe Museum

GEORGIA O'KEEFFE

Santa Fe, USA

Northern New Mexico has a way with people. They stop for a green chile cheeseburger, and find themselves plunking down a deposit on an adobe house a day later. It's the magical light, they'll say. A quality of the sky. The smell of juniper and sage and pinyon pine. It certainly bewitched Georgia

O'Keeffe. Until the late 1920s, O'Keeffe was known mostly for her paintings of skyscrapers and flowers. Then she visited Taos. She'd return every year thereafter, wandering the canyons and silvery mesas, hiking deep into the Jemez Mountains, collecting smooth stones and sun-bleached cow skulls. She bought a house and a ranch in Abiquiú, a tiny village on the Chama River. 'There is nothing to say about it except the fact that for me it is the only place', she wrote her sister. O'Keeffe

© Adam Springer / Shutterstock

died in Santa Fe at 98, having continued to make New Mexico-inspired art until the end of her life. Today, a sprawling adobe complex near Santa Fe's central plaza holds the world's largest collection of her work. Wander the 10 galleries, gazing at her luminous canvasses: smudgy cottonwood trees, desert flowers enlarged to abstraction, curving mesas, blue-green sage. Book ahead to visit her home in Abiquiú, an hour north. And a note on those flower paintings: the photographer Alfred Stieglitz, who became O'Keeffe's husband, mansplained to the world that O'Keeffe's flowers were actually representations of female genitalia. O'Keeffe denied it then – and would deny it for 60 years – but the interpretation stuck. Needless to say, it was a rocky marriage. Perhaps it's time to let the artist have the last word on her own work.

📍 The museum is in Santa Fe. While in New Mexico, it's also possible to tour Ghost Ranch (pictured above), near her home in Abiquiú.

© Graham Hardy / Alamy Stock Photo

St Thomas Churchyard

SYLVIA PLATH

Heptonstall, England

'I took a deep breath and listened to the old bray of my heart. I am. I am. I am.' — *The Bell Jar*

Sylvia Plath (1932-1963) was obsessed with death long before she actually died. Her poems are furious with images of Nazi gas chambers, of hellfire, of sick fragile bodies, of an unlistening God. She attempted suicide several times before she succeeded at age 30. She and her friend, the poet Anne Sexton, 'talked death with burned-up intensity, both of us drawn to it like moths to an electric lightbulb, sucking on it', Sexton recalled.

So while visiting her grave is a bit morbid, it also seems appropriate. Plath is buried in the St Thomas' Churchyard in the village of Heptonstall,

West Yorkshire. Though American, she lived much of her adult life in the UK. She married Ted Hughes, a granite-faced Yorkshire man who wrote burly poems about hawks and moors. Physically and emotionally abusive, he left her for another woman, who would also commit suicide.

Since her death in 1963, Plath defenders have regularly visited Heptonstall to chisel the name 'Hughes' off her gravestone. We suggest bringing her a flower instead, then visiting a local pub to pour one out for one of the 20th century's poetic geniuses.

📍 Heptonstall is in northern England, about equidistant between Manchester and Leeds.

Lahore High Court

ISMAT CHUGHTAI

Lahore, Pakistan

If you ask anyone today about Ismat Chughtai's claim to fame, they'll most likely mention her Urdu story, *Lihaaf* (The Quilt), which rather pointedly refers to a lesbian coupling. Scandalous at the time she wrote it, the story became a battleground. Pages and pages of vituperative hate mail arrived at her door. Scurrilous attacks on its author became common. And in a final stroke of injustice, Chughtai was summoned to the Lahore High Court on a charge of obscenity.

Still, if ever you are summoned to court, you could do worse than Lahore's High Court – built around 1882 (with subsequent additions),

the magnificent building is a jewel of colonial architecture, although notoriously difficult to navigate. Chughtai seemed almost excited to go. She wrote about it rather jauntily in her essay *In the Name of Those Married Women*. 'Everyone said that we would just be fined, not imprisoned. So we were quite excited and began to get warm clothes stitched for our stay in Lahore.'

After her tangle with the law, Chughtai grew into one of the pillars of Urdu fiction, writing short stories and film scripts, and was awarded the prestigious Padma Shri award for distinguished contributions by the Indian government.

📍 The High Court is on Mall Road. Pictured below is the view from Lahore Fort.

Anne Frank House

ANNE FRANK

Amsterdam, Netherlands

'How wonderful it is that nobody need wait a single moment before starting to improve the world.'

Though Anne Frank only found fame after her tragic death, her diary is a triumph of writing for one so young (she began writing it aged 13 in 1942). What she recorded whilst lying low in the secret annex shows maturity of style beyond her years and a passion for a career 'besides having a husband and children'. The power of the diary is amplified by the fact that Frank shared her *achterhuis* (secret annex) hideout not only with her mother, father and sister, but also four others in incredibly cramped conditions, all discovered by German authorities in 1944 and consigned to concentration camps. Frank died there, after enduring terrible hardships, just months before WWII ended.

This information-packed museum solemnly recreates the life of the fugitives during their time in the secret annex through diary extracts and photographs. Easily the most harrowing thing is the fact that this was the very house they hid within.

Trams 13/17 stop at Westermarkt; from here it is a short walk to the Anne Frank House.

© Dennis van de Water / Shutterstock

'When all is said and done, friendship is the only trustworthy fabric of the affections.'

Brindabella Station
MILES FRANKLIN
Brindabella, Australia

Australian writer and feminist Stella Maria Sarah Miles Franklin, aka Miles Franklin (1879–1954), wrote a quintessential coming-of-age story of Australia: *My Brilliant Career* (1901). It contemplates the classic quandary – romantic love and marriage, or the professional satisfactions of a career?

The novel was an immediate success, catapulting the young Franklin into the salons of literary and political Sydney. But further grand success eluded her and she moved to Chicago where she worked at the National Women's Trade Union League and continued to write, often dealing with issues such as women's right to vote and the confines of motherhood. She later worked as a journalist in London and volunteered in Greece during WWI.

Franklin had many suitors but never married. A lifelong supporter of literature and writers, she made a bequest to establish the Miles Franklin Award for the year's best novel or play to present 'Australian life in any of its phases'. In 2013 a second major Australian literary award was named in her honour – the Stella Prize, recognising women writers.

Franklin grew up at Brindabella Station, which she wrote about in *Childhood at Brindabella*. You can stay at Brindabella Station today, in the Snowy Mountains region about an hour's drive from Canberra. A 1901 review of her debut said: 'It is the very first Australian novel to be published ... Her book is a warm embodiment of Australian life, as tonic as bush air, as aromatic as bush trees, and as clear and honest as bush sunlight.'

♥ The 1979 adaptation of *My Brilliant Career* is a good accompaniment to a visit.

© Historical / Getty Images

© Jochen Schlenker / rGetty Images

The Marianne North Tree

MARIANNE NORTH

Warren National Park, Australia

The remote tall forests of Western Australia harbour giant eucalyptus trees with names like poetry – karri, marri, jarrah, tingle. You can drive among them on gravel roads, or walk well-maintained trails that meander through. It wasn't quite so simple when brilliant botanical artist Marianne North visited on the suggestion of her friend Charles Darwin. Travelling by ship, by horse and cart, and by foot, Marianne recorded the landscapes around her. One of her most famous paintings from Western Australia shows an enormous karri tree with a burl rendered with her trademark precision. Astonishingly the tree still exists, protected within Warren National Park near Pemberton. A gracious survivor of the early logging days, it's still known as the Marianne North Tree.

📍 Marianne North's work is on permanent display at the Marianne North Gallery at the Royal Botanic Gardens in Kew, London.

Zora Neale Hurston Museum of Fine Arts

ZORA NEALE HURSTON

Eatonville, USA

The work of celebrated Harlem Renaissance author Zora Neale Hurston (1891–1960) braided eloquent writing with deep human understanding. Though in her later life she was not fully recognised for her extraordinary talent, the late 20th century brought her back to the fore as one of the best chroniclers of life as a black woman, and an inspiration to later generations. Among her best known books are *Their Eyes Were Watching God* and her excellent autobiography *Dust Tracks on a Road*.

📍 Zora Neale Hurston spent her youth in Eatonville, Florida, the first incorporated all-black town in the country. The Zora Neale Hurston Museum of Fine Arts here offers walking tour maps.

Alice Austen House

ALICE AUSTEN

Staten Island, USA

Pretty as a doll's house, the former home of photographer Alice Austen (1866–1952) gazes across to Brooklyn from the shore of Staten Island. Today this bucolic spot is a New York City public park and historic landmark. The house, known as 'Clear Comfort', has been converted into a compelling museum about Austen's life and work.

Arrayed inside the house-museum are photographs from across Austen's impressive career; she produced 8000 in all, though fewer than half have survived. As well as her journalistic assignments, Austen's photographs include images of women playing sports, writing, or draped across chaises longues while dangling cigarettes or goblets of wine from their fingertips. To

Austen, these represented the 'larky life', a way of living that allowed women to embrace their talents freely – counter to established Victorian conventions about women.

As well as perusing her considerable body of work, visitors to the museum can experience an intimate glimpse into Austen's life with her lifelong partner, Gertrude. Objects from around the world, which they collected together, are scattered throughout the museum.

Austen remained a devout gardener even as she suffered from arthritis in later life. Perhaps with this in mind, the landscaped gardens where Austen once held photo shoots are kept immaculate to this day.

To reach the house-museum, board bus S51 or S81 from the St George ferry terminal.

© Katarzyna Musz / Shutterstock

Brontë Parsonage Museum

THE BRONTË SISTERS

Haworth, England

The family home of the trio of sisters (Charlotte, Emily and Anne) that together produced some of the most seminal works in English literature is today much more than a writer's former residence. It is a museum replete with personal effects from the Brontë family: these, displayed in the rooms the sisters once lived and wrote in, offer unparalleled insights into their lives. The surrounding moorland provided many inspirations for the sisters' books, but it was at this handsome house in the West Yorkshire village of Haworth that they spent most of their time and penned most of their prose. Whether it is Charlotte's complex *Villette*, Emily's tragi-romance classic *Wuthering Heights* or Anne's then-controversial *The Tenant of Wildfell Hall*, considered one of the first feminist novels, you can practically feel the literary endeavour oozing from these walls. The Brontes' books did many things to shape the development of literature, not least changing the perception of women in society through their number of strong-willed female protagonists regularly able to out-think, out-act and out-manoeuvre men.

Exploring the Brontë Parsonage Museum, you not only feel closer to a rich vein of literary productivity, but also to the sisters as people rather than writers. The museum is also internationally important for its collection of Brontë texts, and for being one of the oldest literary societies in the world.

📍 The Brontë Bus connects Haworth with Keighley and Hebden Bridge, both of which have railway stations. Fans of *Wuthering Heights* should make the walk up to Top Withens (p85).

Dimbola Lodge

JULIA MARGARET CAMERON

Isle of Wight, England

Home of Victorian photographer Julia Margaret Cameron (1815-1879), Dimbola Lodge is now a museum and gallery dedicated to her life and work. Cameron was a pioneering figure, working with dangerous chemicals in the 'black art' of photography, and subverting the conventions of the time with her conviction that photography was an art form. Experimenting with focus and composition to create some of the finest portraits of her era, Cameron made her home a hub of innovation and the heart of a group of artists known as the Freshwater Circle.

Island Bus No 12 and the FYT bus stop near Dimbola Lodge. You may notice the life-size Jimi Hendrix statue out front first!

Amphlett Lane

CHRISSY AMPHLETT

Melbourne, Australia

In the 1980s, Chrissy Amphlett was Australia's Queen of Rock. The front woman for the guitar-led powerhouse the Divinyls, she made even punk goddess Deborah Harry look like a *Cosmopolitan* cover girl. Chrissy was rawer: her imperfect pout, her power and obvious vulnerability, her boozing and her sexy lyrics. Born in industrial port city Geelong, she is honoured in Melbourne where she once lived with a laneway. Melbourne's city lanes are famous for their intimate bars and street art, so the tribute seems fitting. Chrissy died in 2013 from breast cancer; in 2014 the Cancer Council reinvented her hit 'I Touch Myself' to remind women to check themselves for lumps.

The John Curtain Hotel, a Melbourne gig venue hosting the next generation in Oz rock, is nearby.

Princeton University Firestone Library

TONI MORRISON

Princeton, USA

'If there is a book that you want to read, but it hasn't been written yet, you must be the one to write it.'

Winner of the Pulitzer Prize and the first African American woman to win the Nobel Prize in Literature, writer and professor Toni Morrison (1931-2019) was one of the most important voices of the 20th and 21st centuries. *The Bluest Eye*, *Song of Solomon* and *Beloved*, among other works, explore the black experience with nuance and rich, effortless language that interweaves fiction and poetry. Her work has been adapted to the silver screen (*Beloved*, 1998) and to the opera stage (*Margaret Garner*, 2007), and her words are engraved at the National Memorial for Peace and Justice in Montgomery. It's impossible to overstate Morrison's contribution to American literature, and bibliophiles will delight in tracing her steps through her journey as a writer and educator. Watch the documentary *Toni Morrison: The Pieces I Am* before hitting the road to visit the campuses of Howard University and Cornell University, where Morrison once walked the halls. The big draw, the author's original papers, can be found at Princeton University, where she held the Robert F Goheen Chair in the Humanities. You can also walk past Morrison Hall, named in her honour.

📍 Princeton itself is only a short jaunt from New York City. Make the trip and visit one of NYC's many notable bookstores or hunt down the settings of some of your favourite books.

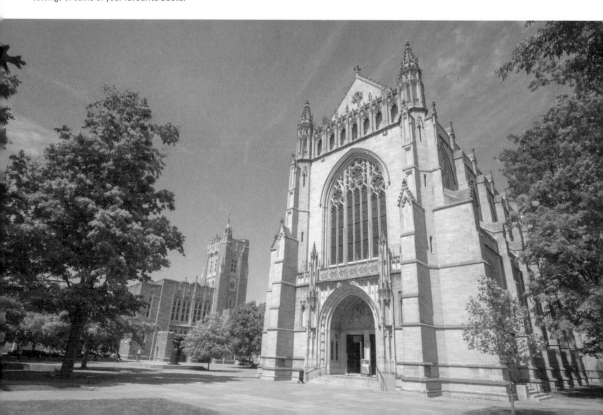

Heydar Aliyev Center

ZAHA HADID

Baku, Azerbaijan

Rising from the ground in a series of mesmerising folds, the shape-shifting Heydar Aliyev Center in Baku opened in 2012 and quickly became recognised as one of the world's most beautiful buildings. Designed by Iraqi-British architect Zaha Hadid (1950–2016), it sits in a large plaza and houses three auditoriums, a museum, a library and an exhibition centre. Its avant-garde design is typical of Hadid, a groundbreaking visual artist whose style defies convention or easy categorisation. Her innovative creations ignore the traditional geometry of construction and instead, rely on fluid, organic curves that offer multiple perspectives. The Heydar Aliyev Center is the best-known example of her style, and walking around its undulating exterior, visitors appreciate the dynamic, sinuous, seamless form.

Famous for her bold architectural statements, Hadid is hailed as one of the foremost architects of her generation. Yet even as she became increasingly well known she stated, 'I will never give myself the luxury of thinking, "I've made it."' In a male-dominated profession, she felt her position to be tenuous: 'As a woman in architecture, you're always an outsider.' The first woman to receive the Pritzker Architecture Prize, architecture's Nobel, she was also twice awarded the Stirling Prize, the UK's most prestigious architectural award, and is the only woman to have been awarded the Royal Gold Medal from the Royal Institute of British Architects. Today, her firm continues to complete her innovative projects posthumously.

📍 Take the red subway line to Nariman Narimanov station, from where the centre is a 15-minute walk.

© ET1972 / Shutterstock; designed by Zaha Hadid Architects

Willa Cather Memorial Prairie

WILLA CATHER

Red Cloud, USA

'As I looked about me I felt that the grass was the country, as the water is the sea.' So spoke the narrator of *My Ántonia*, one of Willa Cather's novels of the Great Plains. Her so-called prairie trilogy brought the immense and isolated West into vivid life, telling stories of settlers and immigrants making a go of the harsh land.

The 612-acre Nebraska grassland dedicated to the author is a fitting memorial to Cather, who grew up here in Red Cloud. The grass has never been plowed, its wildness attracting birds like meadowlarks and prairie chickens.

← The Willa Cather Memorial Prairie is in Red Cloud, southwest of Nebraska's capital, Lincoln.

Blasket Islands

PEIG SAYERS

County Kerry, Ireland

Wild, windswept and remote, the Blasket Islands (Na Blascaodaí) off the Kerry coast were evacuated in 1953 when the final 22 residents moved to the mainland. The harsh reality of island life and its often bleak and brutal twists of fate were immortalised by local *seanchaí* (traditional Irish storyteller) Peig Sayers (1873–1958). Although Peig was illiterate, she dictated her life story to her son Mícheál and it was published, simply entitled *Peig*, in 1936. Recounting near relentless tales of misfortune, this sobering read is a classic title from the Gaelic literary revival.

➡ Ferries run from Ventry, Dunquin and Dingle to the Great Blasket from Easter to October.

Café de Flore

SIMONE DE BEAUVOIR

Paris, France

Beneath the al-fresco canopy at Café de Flore, Parisians and tourists scooch wicker chairs across the paving stones and nibble *pain aux raisins* (raisin-studded pastry) in the sunshine. Inside the cafe, people huddle over their espressos and glasses filled high with chablis and Grand Marnier-fortified champagne. The scene is much the same as when feminist intellectual and philosopher Simone de Beauvoir (1908–1986) haunted the establishment. The cafe was one of her preferred venues for writing, drinking, and having intellectual debates with her partner Jean-Paul Sartre.

De Beauvoir's philosophical texts ruffled feathers with their themes of personal freedom, while her fiction laid bare the tumult of romantic relationships and their aching disappointments. Even those who haven't read her work are familiar with her assertion in *The Second Sex* that 'one is

not born, but rather one becomes a woman' – indeed, the idea that social conditioning shapes gender roles more than biology has evermore resonance today. Many of de Beauvoir's ideas were honed within the walls of Café de Flore: she and Sartre were in the habit of arriving at the cafe each morning to spend an entire day writing here. De Beauvoir lived the freedom that she championed in her written work. Counter to societal expectations, she neither married nor had any children. Although she and Sartre were emotionally devoted to one another, they each freely pursued other affairs. Her sharp intellect and talent for rendering human experiences in raw, yet understated prose continue to mark her out as one of France's most legendary writers; no wonder, then, that her legacy is part of what draws visitors to the Café de Flore's art deco interior.

The cafe is a few steps away from the Saint-Germain-des-Prés station (metro line 4).

© tunart / Getty Images

'I paint and collect mundane feelings, thoughts and words. I am trying to capture the life of the soul.'

Chernobyl Exclusion Zone

SVETLANA ALEXEIVICH

Pripyat, Ukraine

In the aftermath of a reactor explosion in 1986, cities and villages were abandoned. Decades on, tourists can visit Chernobyl (or Chornobyl as it's called here) to find an eerie landscape of crumbling buildings being reclaimed by nature. Many will have had their interest piqued by the HBO miniseries of the same name, but fans of 2015 Nobel Prize in Literature winner Svetlana Alexeivich may be drawn to the abandoned village of Pripyat based on her oral history about the disaster. Her lyrical interviews with firefighters, physicists, recovery workers and local residents make the tragedy incredibly vivid. Belarusian Alexeivich's astounding books take firsthand testimony about the recent history of the former USSR and turn it into art, creating a new form of so-called documentary literature. Each book is imprinted with her interest in human suffering and her preference for lived experience over idealism.

📍 Travels throughout the former USSR are best done with *Second-hand Time* and *The Unwomanly Face of War* as reading material.

Laura Ingalls Cabin

LAURA INGALLS WILDER

Pepin, USA

Pack up your china shepherdess and hitch up your wagon: You're going to the house of Laura Ingalls Wilder (1867-1957) in Pepin, Wisconsin – or, to be more accurate, a very charming replica of it. This 'little house in the big woods' is built in the same place as the original and gives fans of Wilder's *Little House on the Prairie* series a glimpse of what it was like in 1867 when Laura was born there.

There are many fascinating Laura Ingalls Wilder sites throughout the Midwest, each with their own collections of varying interest and breadth, but the Little House Wayside Cabin is where it all began. Faithful readers will be able to close their eyes and imagine Wilder's nostalgic scenes of Pa and Ma as they struggled to raise their children in what was once the frontier.

📍 The town of Pepin hosts 'Laura Ingalls Wilder Days' every September in honour of her (under debate) legacy.

© John D. Ivanko / Alamy Stock Photo

Farleys House and Gallery
LEE MILLER
Sussex, England

If you're a female shutterbug, there's a good chance that one of your heroines is Lee Miller, a *Vogue* model who became Man Ray's muse and collaborator, then a war photographer. Embedded with the US army in WWII, Miller was present at the liberation of Dachau and said she could never get the stench of it out of her nostrils. After the war she retreated to Farleys farmhouse in the Sussex countryside, where she entertained Picasso, Joan Miró and Max Ernst (who helped out in the garden) and became an accomplished chef. Visitors would often give a sketch or painting, leaving the colourful farmhouse walls decked out with masterpieces. It now houses the Lee Miller archive.

⬅ Non-drivers can take a train to Lewes and cycle to Farleys in around an hour.

Ingrid Jonker Memorial
INGRID JONKER
Gordon's Bay, South Africa

The memorial to Ingrid Jonker's (1933-1965), a silver-painted sculpture of a tricycle with a pair of sandals hanging from the handlebars, sits in her childhood home of Gordon's Bay. The lines on the concrete plinth are from her 1960 poem 'The child who was shot dead by soldiers at Nyanga'. The Afrikaans poet wrote the poem in response to police brutality in Cape Town's Nyanga township, during anti-apartheid protests that culminated in the Sharpeville massacre. Jonker's short, tumultuous life (later depicted in the film *Black Butterflies)* ended in suicide, but three decades later Nelson Mandela read her poem about the child during his inaugural presidential address.

➡ From Gordon's Bay, one of the world's most beautiful coastal roads, Route 44, leads down the eastern shore of False Bay.

119

'There are as many sorts of women as there are women.' –*The Tale of Genji*

Kiyomizu-dera

MURASAKI SHIKIBU

Kyoto, Japan

Murasaki Shikibu, the author of *The Tale of Genji*, considered the world's first novel, wrote from a position of privilege as lady-in-waiting to the empress. Her epic narrative, completed circa 1012 AD, was written in kana (as opposed to in Chinese characters, the script used by male officials), indicating that it was meant for a mainly female readership. The saga follows the Imperial Court's favoured son Prince Genji through his many love affairs as he criss-crosses the Heian capital of Kyoto to attend festivals, woo potential lovers and visit temples, all rituals of state intimately familiar to his author.

One such temple was Kiyomizu-dera in the hills of Higashiyama. The ancient temple here was first built in 798 and would have been familiar to the fictional Genji and his creator, though the present buildings are reconstructions dating from 1633. Today it has become one of the most famous landmarks of Kyoto. In a city that offers tantalising hints of Genji and Murasaki Shikibu's Heian-era Japan around every corner and yet which has been remade by natural disasters multiple times over its history, Kiyomizu-dera is a rare chance to glimpse a place of worship used by Kyoto residents for over a millennium.

📍 All but the most ambitious readers may want to stick to the first book of *The Tale of Genji*, which spans over 1000 pages at its full length.

Boston Women's Memorial

PHILLIS WHEATLEY

Boston, USA

The path she walked through life was far from typical, yet Phillis Wheatley became one of the most celebrated US poets of the 18th century. She was born in Gambia/Senegal in about 1753 and enslaved and transported to the American colonies. On arriving in Boston in 1761 she was bought for a pittance by the Wheatley family, who wanted a household servant. They named her Phillis, after the boat she arrived on. Unusually, the Wheatley family taught Phillis to read and, obviously brilliant, Phillis learned Greek, Latin, and studied the Bible and the British canon. She also learned history, geography and astronomy and thirsted for a more academic setting. Nevertheless, the Wheatleys would not grant her freedom until 1773, just before the woman of the house, Susanna Wheatley, died.

While living enslaved, Phillis Wheatley wrote poetry, starting as an early teen and later travelling to England to present her work. Abolitionists and prominent figures such as John Hancock vouched for her, to prove that she was, indeed, the author of these classically styled works inspired by biblical and elegiac imagery and forms. Her 1773 collection *Poems on Various Subjects, Religious and Moral* was the first book published by an African writer in America. She wrote prolifically and achieved fame on both sides of the Atlantic, but would die in poverty at age 31 during childbirth, struggling to support herself, the Wheatleys leaving her nothing after their deaths. Today the Boston Women's Memorial on Commonwealth Avenue honours Wheatley, shown against its stone pedestal as if deep in thought.

📍 Abigail Adams and Lucy Stone are also honoured here.

PHILLIS WHEATLEY

© Jorge Salcedo / Shutterstock, sculptor © Meredith Bergmann

Museo Deleddiano

GRAZIA DELEDDA

Sardinia, Italy

Nobel-prize winning Sardinian author Grazie Deledda received the basic schooling of her era: 4 years. But a young Deledda began writing from an early age, despite all the impediments to being a woman of letters. Born in 1871 in Nuoro, a mountain town in the heart of the Barbagia region of Sardinia, she used the rough and wild landscape of her homeland as a metaphor and backdrop to her dramatic stories, novels, plays and poems. A prolific author, Deledda gained renown in her lifetime as a leading proponent of the *verismo* (realism) school of Italian literature and was

awarded the Nobel Prize for Literature in 1926 — the first Italian woman to receive the prize.

Today, you can visit her first home at the Museo Deleddiano in Nuoro where she lived from her birth to her marriage in 1900. This simple three-story stone building edged by a tall wall transports you back in time with its period furnishings — from Deledda's writing desk to tidy internal courtyards in which she played. Journey into her imagination with a priceless collection of photos, period documents, manuscripts and the personal belongings of the writer.

Make a pilgrimage to Deledda's burial place at the nearby Chiesa della Madonna della Solitudine on the edge of Nuoro.

Skala Eresou
SAPPHO
Lesvos (Mytilini), Greece

An ancient Greek poet from the island of Lesvos, Sappho's writing only survives in fragments. Often sung by one person accompanied by a lyre, it featured grand passions and erotic contemplations, often of other women. Besides the few fragments dating to the 6th century BC, little is known of her life except that she ran an academy to educate unmarried young women devoted to the cults of Eros and Aphrodite. The mystery has only made her poetry more evocative. She has a rich modern-day following, her fame perhaps partly fanned by the reputation that derived the word 'lesbian' from the name of her island, Lesvos. Home to the village of Skala Eresou, where Sappho was born, it also produces some of Greece's finest olive oil and ouzo.

Modern poet Anne Carson's 2003 reinterpretation of Sappho's fragments, *If Not, Winter*, is a good place to start reading the ancient Greek poet.

'Truth isn't always beauty,
but the hunger for it is.'

Constitution Hill
NADINE GORDIMER
Johannesburg, South Africa

When Nadine Gordimer (1923–2014) accepted the Nobel Prize for Literature in 1991, becoming the first South African and the first woman in 25 years to win the award, the then 68-year-old used her speech to call for continued economic sanctions against South Africa. This was typical of the single-minded novelist, who tirelessly campaigned against the injustices of apartheid in both word and deed, openly supporting Nelson Mandela's ANC (African National Congress) and other organisations banned by the repressive apartheid government. Gordimer even edited Mandela's famous 'I am prepared to die' speech, delivered in court before his long incarceration, and the future president said reading her books in prison taught him 'a great deal about the liberal white sensibility'.

However, Gordimer was more than a protest writer, and her stories cover all the nuances and neuroses of life in a racially divided society, turning a critical eye to the brutality of racism and the hypocrisies of liberals alike. Compared to the likes of Toni Morrison and Alice Walker for melding the personal and the political, Gordimer's best-known novels include *July's People* and *Burgher's Daughter*, both written during the aftermath of the 1976 Soweto uprising, and the 1974 Booker Prize winner, *The Conservationist*.

With an unconventional style typified by Proustian sentences and fragments, Gordimer was equally critical of the crime and corruption that blight post-apartheid South Africa. In Johannesburg, where Gordimer spent most of her life, visit Constitution Hill, home to the new Constitutional Court and an apartheid-era prison, to see both the ideals she treasured and the forces she battled.

📍 Constitution Hill is in central Johannesburg, 1.5km (1 mi) north of Park Station, and best reached by car.

'My dreams were all my own; I accounted for them to nobody; they were my refuge when annoyed - my dearest pleasure when free.'

Villa Diodati

MARY SHELLEY

Lake Geneva, Switzerland

It was a dark and stormy night...

No, but really. 1816 has been called the 'Year Without a Summer'. A volcanic eruption in Indonesia the previous year had shot ash into the atmosphere, sending global temperatures plummeting. It was June on Lake Geneva, but icy, whipping rain drove Lord Byron and his friends inside the rented villa, where they huddled by the fire, entertaining themselves by reading ghost stories aloud. Eventually they decided to make a contest of writing their own spooky tales.

The hands-down winner was the unconventional 18-year-old Mary Wollstonecraft Godwin (1797-1851), daughter of the trailblazing feminist writer Mary Wollstonecraft and the anarchist philosopher William Godwin. Inspired by a nightmare, she told a tale of a mad scientist who defies nature to create a hideous creature. The name of the scientist (not the creature) was Frankenstein.

Frankenstein; or, The Modern Prometheus was published in 1818 on the heels of that competition.

It has never gone out of print since. The smash novel's author would go on to wed her then-married lover from that summer, the poet Percy Bysshe Shelley, who later drowned in a sailing accident at 29. They'd have four children together, but only one would live to adulthood. She published many more books, worked as an editor, championed Percy's posthumous legacy, and helped fellow women in need.

Today, the Villa Diodati that hosted Mary Shelley and Lord Byron has been converted to private luxury apartments. But much of Lake Geneva remains unchanged from the wild summer of 1816 when Byron and his circle of Romantics sailed the stormy waters, hiked the glaciers and rambled through the ruined castles. Visit the Gothic cathedrals of Lausanne; buy cheese in the ancient stone villages dotting the corners of the lake; trek into the deep, cool gorges; swim as the late afternoon sun turns the navy water a golden peach; and read *Frankenstein* in its proper setting.

📍 Geneva itself boasts a hulking sculpture of Frankenstein in the Plainpalais neighbourhood.

Abbey Theatre

LADY GREGORY

Dublin, Ireland

Once upon a time, if you desired any sort of standing in the Irish literary world, you were best off going through Augusta, otherwise known as Lady Gregory (1852–1932): folklorist, playwright, and mother of the Irish Literary Revival. Her home of Coole Park was a gathering place for writers including WB Yeats, whose patron she was, and she worked untiringly to support Irish culture.

The tireless Lady Gregory used her now-demolished home as a gathering place for the best in Irish fairytales, books and minds, helping to revive the Irish language and reignite a culture that had been nearly snuffed out by English rule. While bureaucrats saw to it that Coole Park didn't survive, the Abbey Theatre she co-founded still serves as a stage for productions in Dublin. If Irish culture is alive and well today, it is in large part due to the efforts of Lady Gregory.

If you do visit Coole Park, wear comfortable shoes so you can hike all around the remaining grounds. Seek out the 'autograph tree' with the initials of the biggest names in Irish literature including George Bernard Shaw, JM Synge, Augustus John, WB Yeats, and Lady Gregory herself.

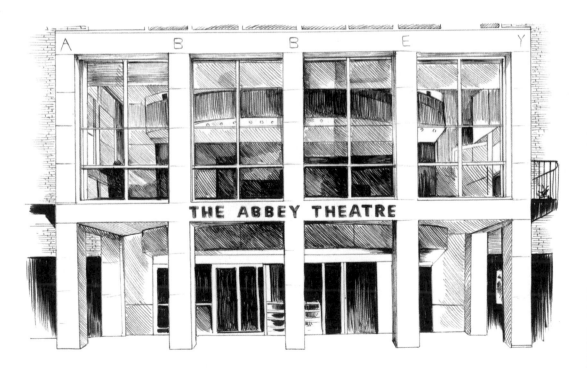

San Francisco Main Library
MAYA ANGELOU
San Francisco, USA

The celebrated poet and novelist Maya Angelou (1928-2014) is slated to return to her one-time home of San Francisco as a new monument — part of the city's plan to close the gender gap between public art representing historical men and women. The late writer and civil rights activist had strong ties to the Golden Gate city. She attended Washington High School, worshipped at Glide Church, and became San Francisco's first African American female streetcar conductor.

The author of *I Know Why the Caged Bird Sings* is considered one of America's greatest literary icons and a champion of the autobiographical form. The aforementioned novel describes Angelou's abusive childhood and rocky entrance into adolescence as a teenager in the Bay Area. After working as a streetcar conductor, she later became a fry cook, sex worker, actor, journalist, lecturer, and leader of the Civil Rights Movement. In 2010 Angelou received the Presidential Medal of Freedom for her lifetime achievements, the nation's highest civilian award.

After whittling down the competition from 100 submissions, San Francisco's Arts Commission announced an official selection for the monument's design in September 2019 with the forthcoming statue slated for installation at the city's main library by the end of 2020.

The main library is close to the Civic Center BART stop and accessible by the Market St streetcar. Above, a proposed design by Lava Thomas.

© Petr Kovalenkov / Shutterstock

Théâtre de la Ville

SARAH BERNHARDT

Paris, France

Sarah Bernhardt (1844–1923) was born Henriette-Rosine Bernard, but her nickname once she became the greatest French actress of the late 19th century was the Divine Sarah. Propelled into the theatre by one of her mother's lovers, Bernhardt spent part of her early career at the Comédie-Française. She also worked for years at the Odéon Theatre, and in 1870, during the Franco-German War, she organised a military hospital there. One of the most celebrated actresses ever on stage, she also had her own theatre company at the height of her career and toured the world.

← The theatre in Paris that Bernhardt managed and renamed the Théâtre Sarah Bernhardt is now known as the Théâtre de la Ville.

Smekkleysa Plötubúð (Bad Taste)

BJÖRK

Reykjavik, Iceland

Officially born Björk Guðmundsdóttir (her last name is a patronymic), Björk has risen to fame throughout the world for her eclectic blend of punk, new wave, electronica and experimental pop. Her videos, costumes and imagery for her albums are as fascinating as the avant-garde music she makes, so much so that New York's Metropolitan Museum of Art held a grand retrospective of Björk's myriad works of art in 2015. She first found international fame with the band The Sugarcubes, whose home base was the Reykjavík arts collective Smekkleysa Plötubúð, a record label that remains a creative haven.

➡ Record store Smekkleysa Plötubúð can be found on Skólavörðurstígur 16, entry on Óðinsgata (closed on Sundays).

© Santiago Felipe / Getty Images

Dove Cottage

DOROTHY WORDSWORTH

Grasmere, England

Dove Cottage in the sweepingly scenic Lake District of England is a place of pilgrimage for lovers of the work of William Wordsworth. A good proportion of these pilgrims are also in search of his sister Dorothy (1771–1855), who was herself a poet and more notably a brilliant diarist. William fell in love with slate-roofed, lime-washed Dove Cottage in 1799, and set up a beguiling but austere home with his wife and children as well as sister Dorothy. Together William and Dorothy created the steep fell-side garden, entertained visitors such as Coleridge and Thomas De Quincy, and wrote. Dorothy's output became known as the *Grasmere Journal*, a log of artistic friendships, a document of rural life, a vital record of conversations with William and a contemplation of the natural world.

Dorothy's write-up of an ascent of Scafell Pike was wrongly attributed to William in a popular guide to the Lake District but William had the highest opinion of his sister's sensitive observations, writing: 'she gave me eyes, she gave me ears'. Dorothy wrote of a belt of daffodils they encountered together that 'tossed and reeled and danced and seemed as if they verily laughed with the wind that blew upon them over the lake, they looked so gay ever glancing ever changing'. Two years later William's most celebrated poem echoed his sister's lovely words.

The nearest train station is Windermere – regular buses run from there to Grasmere.

Jane Austen House Museum

JANE AUSTEN

Chawton, England

For most 18th-century women, a good marriage was the ultimate goal in life. Jane Austen (1775-1817) had other ideas however, turning down a marriage proposal and instead choosing to work and earn her own living. It was a courageous choice; the few female authors of the time were considered lewd and scandalous, the more ambitious publishing under a male pseudonym.

Indeed, Austen titled her first novel, *Sense and Sensibility*, as 'By a Lady'. Her character Elizabeth, in *Pride and Prejudice*, comes close to explaining her situation: 'There is a stubbornness about me that never can bear to be frightened at the will of others. My courage always rises at every attempt to intimidate me.' At the time it was a gamble, and when *Pride and Prejudice* came out in 1831, an early critic declared it 'much too clever to have been written by a woman'.

Austen lived with her mother and sister in a modest red-brick 17th-century house in the village of Chawton from 1809 until her death in 1817. While living here, she wrote *Mansfield Park*, *Emma* and *Persuasion,* and revised *Sense and Sensibility*, *Pride and Prejudice* and *Northanger Abbey.* Walking through the house, you get a sense of the very prim and proper society of the time. You can see her tiny walnut writing desk, her bookcase now filled with early editions of her novels, her surviving letters, jewellery and clothing. While here, you can dress in Regency clothes, make a lavender bag or wander the garden as Jane almost certainly did. It's a literary pilgrimage with special significance for her fans, known as 'Janeites'.

⚲ Take bus 64 from Winchester to Chawton Roundabout (45 minutes, hourly), then walk to Chawton village.

© Dmitry Naumov / Shutterstock

©FrankvandenBergh / Getty Images

'It isn't where you came from; it's where you're going that counts.'

Apollo Theater

ELLA FITZGERALD

Harlem, USA

When the Apollo Theater first lit its glittering marquee in 1934, it transformed what had previously been an exclusively white burlesque stage into the most vital venue for African American performance in America. Embedded in the heart of Harlem, nearly all the most legendary soul and jazz artists of the 20th century played the Apollo's magnificent Jazz Age mainstage, among them Duke Ellington, Sam Cooke, Ray Charles and Stevie Wonder. Although the Apollo was initially unusual in its emphasis on African American performers, its audiences were far from exclusively black: many white music-lovers made their way to the Apollo in its early years to hear the best music New York had to offer.

The Apollo is perhaps most renowned for its Amateur Nights, a weekly talent competition that continues to this day. Many musical artists have gotten their start at Amateur Night at the Apollo, including Billie Holiday and Aretha Franklin, but the most celebrated victor remains the First Lady of Song, Ella Fitzgerald (1917-1996), who won one of the first competitions when she was only 17 years old. It was a sign of greatness to come. From here the Queens native went on to forge her own unique style, leaving a monumental legacy that spanned six decades.

The Apollo Theater is still in operation; stop by the box office to see a show.

Whitehall Hotel

EDNA ST VINCENT MILLAY

Camden, USA

Edna St Vincent Millay (1892-1950) couldn't wait to leave Camden. The young poet, who called herself 'Vincent', thought she was bound for bigger things than small town Maine. She was. Edna would live in Greenwich Village during the wild days of the early Jazz Age. She would sail for Paris as a foreign correspondent for *Vanity Fair*. She would become the first woman to win the Pulitzer for poetry. She would picket for Communist causes and write impassioned anti-Nazi verse. She would take and discard lovers of both sexes everywhere she went.

But the rocky coast of Maine was her heart. It was here that her indomitable mother raised three daughters in a home with little money but plenty of literature and song. A teenage Millay was reciting poetry at a Camden hotel when she caught the eye of Caroline Dow, a wealthy New Yorker, who became her patron. That hotel still stands. It's called the Whitehall, whose columned porch is one of the world's truly great places for relaxing, the salty tang of Penobscot Bay in your nostrils. The summit of nearby Mount Battie inspired Millay to compose her poem *Renascence*, which begins: 'All I could see from where I stood was three long mountains and a wood. I turned and looked another way and saw three islands in a bay'.

 Camden is on Maine's midcoast, just under 2 hours driving time from Portland. Above, the harbour view from Mount Battie.

© Orhan Cam / Shutterstock

Lincoln Memorial

MARIAN ANDERSON

Washington, DC, USA

One of the most celebrated singers of the 20th century, Marian Anderson (1897–1993) showed immense musical talent from early childhood. She was given formal vocal training when her family's church congregation pitched in so she could have lessons. Her father bought her a piano and she taught herself to play.

A pure contralto with an enormous range and a rich tone, Anderson would become a celebrated singer both in the US and abroad. She faced myriad barriers due to her race, but was invited to perform at the White House by Franklin and Eleanor Roosevelt. In 1930, when Anderson was barred from singing due to racist policies at Washington, DC's Constitution Hall, Eleanor Roosevelt invited her to sing at the Lincoln Memorial instead. One of Anderson's most iconic performances, to an integrated audience of over 75,000 people and broadcast live to millions on the radio, it helped set the stage for the civil rights era to come. Anderson was also the first African American artist to perform with the New York Metropolitan Opera, In 1955.

Her fame continued to grow and she would go on to perform at the inauguration of John F Kennedy, and he would later award her the Presidential Medal of Freedom, the highest civilian honour in the US. She also worked as a delegate for the United Nations Human Rights Committee, tireless in her pursuit of justice.

In addition to visiting the Lincoln Memorial, the site of Marian Anderson's famous concert, you can also now watch it online.

Mahasweta Devi Museum

MAHASWETA DEVI

Kolkata, India

The first time you read Mahasweta Devi's writing, it can feel as if someone has picked you up and shaken you by the shoulders. For if anyone ever wielded their words as a weapon, it was Mahasweta Devi, who tore into cosy middle-class morality and an unjust political system that dragged down those on the crumbling fringes of India – the subaltern, the dispossessed, the forest dwellers, and indigenous peoples of India.

Devi was an activist, a teacher, but most of all a writer: her books, written in Bengali, were translated into English and other Indian regional languages and were then turned into plays and films. National and international awards came fast and thick (including the Ramon Magsaysay Award in 1997, and a nomination for the Man Booker in 2009). She shrugged all the plaudits off. Instead she distilled her activist gaze on atrocities against tribes, strongly opposing the West Bengal government's policies of stripping indigenous people of their land.

In Mahasweta Devi's beautifully maintained museum in south Kolkata, you'll see the thinker behind the woman. Her home between 2011-2015, it is now filled with her manuscripts, books, articles, awards and a whole slew of gifts that came her way from scholars and literati right up until her death in 2016.

📍 This isn't on Google maps, so it's a bit of a run-around, but your work is done once you find the Gate Academy on Rajdanga main road. The house is almost opposite.

School of Northwest Coast Art

FREDA DIESING

Terrace, Canada

Freda Diesing (1925–2002) was one of the first female Haida woodcarvers and was a major player in the resurgence and consequent widespread appreciation of Native Canadian northwest art and culture in the 1960s. Named Skil Kew Wat (Magical Little Woman) in the Haida language, Freda was indeed a magical-feeling person who started her career at age 42 and went on to become one of the region's most renowned carvers as well as a mentor and teacher. It's only fitting that the only school that focuses on First Nations Pacific Northwestern art is named in her honour.

◄ See massive bears in their natural habitat at Khutzeymateen Grizzly Bear Sanctuary nearby.

The Owl House

HELEN MARTINS

Nieu Bethesda, South Africa

In the unlikely setting of a secluded village in a remote corner of the Karoo semi-desert is a striking piece of 'outsider' art, a cottage turned into a surreal, poignant and at times disturbing artwork by the late Helen Martins. Finding herself back in her isolated hometown after a failed marriage, she set about filling her cottage and garden with hundreds of life-sized decorated concrete figures. Silent rows of camels, mermaids, nativity scenes and trademark owls were made by Martins, who took her own life in 1976. Undeterred by her conservative community's disapproval, Martins pursued her vision and posthumously turned Nieu Bethesda into an arts destination.

➡ Athol Fugard's play The Road to Mecca tells Martin's story.

12

FEMINIST BOOKSTORES

Feminist bookstores have been around since the heyday of the women's movement, and are currently experiencing a renaissance.

—

1 A ROOM OF ONE'S OWN Madison, USA

This expansive, politically active shop can be found just outside the University of Wisconsin, Madison, and caters to the college's population.

2 BLUESTOCKINGS New York City, USA

This volunteer-run radical and feminist bookstore in Manhattan's Lower East Side carries new and used books along with an extensive collection of zines.

3 BOOKWOMAN Austin, USA

Founded in the 1970s, this cosy, queer-friendly shop is a mainstay of feminist culture in Austin. Its specialties include poetry, feminism and children's books.

4 CHARIS BOOKS Decatur, USA

The oldest feminist bookshop in America and a bastion of lesbian activism in Georgia, Charis Books (now in Decatur) sells progressive books for adults and children.

5 LIBRAIRIE L'EUGUÉLIONNE Montreal, Canada

Located in the heart of Montreal's Gay Village, this bright, welcoming shop specialises in feminist and queer books, and stocks both new and used titles in French and English.

6 LIBRERÍA DE MUJERES Buenos Aires, Argentina

The only feminist bookshop in Argentina features over 30,000 titles, and operates a small press which has published children's books and essays on feminist topics.

7 · LIBRERÍA MUJERES Madrid, Spain

Conveniently located just off the Plaza Mayor, Madrid's only feminist bookstore, with the motto 'Books don't bite, neither does feminism', features books by women across genres for all ages.

8 · PERSEPHONE BOOKS London, UK

This small, chic shop in central London is the storefront outpost of Persephone Books, a small press that publishes high-quality reissues of neglected works by women writers.

9 · THE SECOND SHELF London, UK

Specialising in rare and antiquarian editions of books by and about women, this tiny, vibrant Soho bookshop also carries affordable editions for burgeoning collectors.

10 · VIOLETTE AND CO Paris, France

Located between the Place de la Bastille and Père Lachaise Cemetery, this shop features a wide range of queer and feminist titles. Its second floor is dedicated to its extensive event program.

11 · THE WOMEN'S BOOKSHOP Auckland, NZ

You can find both new, mainstream and more niche feminist titles by women in this friendly shop in Auckland, which boasts a particularly strong travel section.

12 · WOMEN & CHILDREN FIRST Chicago, USA

With over 30,000 books in stock and a full events calendar, this bookshop has been a central feature of the city's feminist and literary scenes since its founding in 1979.

PATH-BREAKERS

'I still vote civilisation a nuisance, society a humbug and all conventionality a crime.'

Rocky Mountain National Park

ISABELLA BIRD

Colorado, USA

If the adage 'never judge a book by a cover' ever needed a face, consider that of Isabella Bird (1831-1904). Raised in England, she stood under five feet tall and spent much of her 72 years ignoring various illnesses by travelling to and writing about the world's furthest corners (New Zealand, Japan, Persia and Colorado's Rockies). Her 1879 memoir *A Lady's Life in the Rocky Mountains* is an all-time classic. Travelling in her 40s by pony en route back from the Sandwich Islands, she rode deep into Colorado's wild, settling at last in an Estes Park cabin above a family of skunks. Today it's much visited; in 1873 only a handful of 'desperadoes' lived in the area, including a one-eyed trapper she seemed to fall for. To Bird's amazed eye, the pines, valleys and glacial-carved mountains dripped in colour. Rocks become 'blood red' and 'carmine', while Longs Peak, a 14,000-foot summit she climbed in a skirt, is a 'landmark in purple glory'. (It may have inspired the 'purple mountain majesties' line from Katharine Lee Bates' 1895 poem 'America the Beautiful'.) That elusive majestic colour can still be found in Rocky Mountain National Park in the same spots that awed in the 1800s. Take the roads at dusk, admiring the views. Isabella Bird was onto a good thing.

 During the winter, visitation drops by nearly 90% when compared with the bumper-to-bumper traffic in summer.

Escape Ella Maillart

ELLA MAILLART

Chandolin, Switzerland

Although she was on the Swiss National Ski Team and represented Switzerland in sailing at the 1924 Paris Olympics, Ella Maillart (1903-1997) is best known as a traveller and for her extraordinary seven-month trek across China from Beijing to Kashmir in 1935. Kini to her friends, she wrote about the trip in *Forbidden Journey,* but the epic crossing is equally interesting for her companion Peter Fleming's contrasting account. She wrote that 'To dawdle is my usual fashion, as if I had the whole of eternity before me.' Peter, older brother of James Bond creator Ian Fleming, was decidedly in a hurry and wrote about it in *News from Tartary.*

Later she travelled and wrote from Turkey, Iran and Afghanistan, driving with another woman from Geneva to Kabul, Afghanistan, in 1939. WWII interrupted her travels and she spent the war years studying Hindu philosophy in India. The war over, she returned to Switzerland and for the next 50 years spent half of each year in the mountain village of Chandolin. As the village's most famous resident she even has her own museum in the chapel of Sainte-Barbe, which displays brilliant photographs from the world explorations of this woman who wrote 'you do not travel if you are afraid of the unknown, you travel for the unknown'.

📍 The intrepid traveller is also recognised in the Ella Maillart wing of the Karakol Historical Museum in Kyrgyzstan; her book *Turkestan Solo* explored the region.

© Andre Jenny / Alamy Stock Photo

© A. Y. Owen / Getty Images

Five Moons Statue

MARIA TALLCHIEF

Tulsa, USA

Maria Tallchief (1925–2013) moved to New York City aged just 17 to pursue her ballet dreams. Born Elizabeth Marie Tall Chief, with a father who was a member of the Osage Nation, she started training at an early age and became the country's first true prima ballerina. In 1947, she became the first American to dance with the Paris Opera Ballet and in 1960 was the first to dance at Moscow's Bolshoi Theater. Her then-husband, George Balanchine of the New York City Ballet, created roles just for her, and she performed alongside Rudolf Nureyev and later founded Chicago City Ballet. Tallchief steadfastly spoke out against discrimination toward Native Americans and is honoured by the Five Moons statue at the Tulsa Historical Society garden in her home state of Oklahoma.

💡 Visitors to Tulsa with an interest in dance can also check out the performance schedule of the Tulsa Ballet.

© shaunl / Getty mages

Nova Scotia College of Art & Design

ANNA LEONOWENS

Halifax, Canada

Over the years you may have felt that Anna Leonowens (1831-1915) has been following you, since snippets of her history seem to turn up everywhere. Most people know Anna as the governess of King Mongkut of Siam's children in modern-day Thailand, who inspired the story for *The King and I*. But teaching in Siam was only a blip of her well-travelled life; you might find stories of her from Singapore to New York City. Towards the end of her life, she settled in Halifax, Nova Scotia, and helped found the Nova Scotia College of Art and Design. Stepping into the Anna Leonowens Gallery within the college is a fitting memorial to her adventurous, feminist and artistic soul.

💡 The nearby Local Council of Women, once led by Leonowens, is in a visit-worthy Queen Anne style building.

© Pictorial Parade / Getty Images

Shirley Chisholm State Park

SHIRLEY CHISHOLM

Brooklyn, USA

The political career of Shirley Chisholm (1924–2005) career was a cascade of firsts. First African American woman elected to the US Congress, first African American candidate for president for a major US political party, and first woman to run for the Democratic party's presidential nomination.

In the early part of her political career, she was a Democratic senator in the New York Legislature, and when she joined the US Congress, she served in the US House of Representatives for a whopping seven terms, from 1969 to 1983. Among her legions of accomplishments while in office, Chisholm was key in the formation of the Special Supplemental

Nutrition Program for Women, Infants and Children (WIC) program which provides food to women and children in need to this day. She also championed the rights of domestic workers to be paid a minimum wage. And not only that: the entire staff of Chisholm's congressional office was female, and half were African American.

The first phase of the 407-acre Shirley Chisholm State Park named in her honour opened to the public in 2019. Located in her home borough of Brooklyn, the park is the largest state park in New York City and its first phase has 16 km (10 mi) of hiking and walking trails.

At the park's high point, enjoy views from the Verrazzano–Narrows Bridge to the Empire State Building and Jamaica Bay.

Clinton House Museum

HILLARY RODHAM CLINTON

Fayetteville, USA

© mauritius images GmbH / Alamy Stock Photo

The 1930s brick house peers down at Clinton Drive, a stretch of road in Fayetteville, Arkansas, that was called California Boulevard before Hillary Rodham Clinton and her husband Bill came along. Your free tour begins in the living room where the two were married in 1975 surrounded by family and friends. You can see a replica of Hillary's dress, which she bought for $53 at the mall the day before the wedding, mostly at the insistence of her mother. Unconventional from the start, Hillary didn't want an engagement ring nor the ceremonial fanfare, and she long refused to take Bill's last name.

You'll also see the room she and Bill used as a library with bookshelves made out of cinder blocks and pieces of wood. While she lived in Fayetteville, Hillary taught at the University of Arkansas School of Law just up the hill from her home. In that time, she became the director of a new legal aid clinic at the school and helped found the city's first rape crisis centre. Although Hillary only lived at 930 W Clinton Drive for a year and a half, it was a pivotal part of her journey to becoming a political powerhouse whose influence has been felt around the world.

From the Fayetteville Square go west on Center St until it becomes Clinton Drive.

Cappoquin Library

DERVLA MURPHY

Cappoquin, Ireland

Pedalling her first bicycle, 10-year-old Dervla mused 'if I went on doing this for long enough I could get to India.' She remained at home looking after her parents until her early 30s when, straddling Roz, the bicycle she named after Don Quixote's faithful steed Rocinante, she rode out of Lismore in 1963. *Full Tilt: Ireland to India with a Bicycle*, the book that trip inspired, has never been out of print and is still the best ever account of the joys and hardships of a good long bike ride.

Dervla's subsequent life has been similarly full tilt, travelling hard and doing it tough, whether it was *In Ethiopia with a Mule, On a Shoestring to Coorg* or in countries and regions as varied as Nepal, Tibet, Baltistan, Siberia, Peru, Cameroon and Madagascar. Later her writing took on a distinctly political stance as she visited and wrote about Northern Ireland, Palestine and Gaza, Cuba, Zimbabwe and the Balkans, confronting subjects as wide ranging as globalisation, nuclear power and climate change.

For many years Roz was on display pinned to the wall of the Lismore Public Library (below), but recently she moved to the library in Cappoquin, where the hardy bike can be seen during the weekly opening hours.

It's a relatively short jaunt from Cappoquin to Lismore Castle's gardens.

Manhattan Project National Historical Park

CHIEN-SHIUNG WU

Los Alamos, USA

'First lady of physics' Chien-Shiung Wu worked on isolating uranium isotopes as part of the Manhattan Project, but her influence on experimental physics extends much further (see the experiment bearing her name). She won the inaugural Wolf Prize in 1978, and contributed to Nobel Prize-winning breakthroughs. Born in China in 1912, she was an exemplary student as well as an activist and went on to receive a PhD from the University of Wisconsin. Each site at the Los Alamos national historical park spotlights a different aspect of the development of the atomic bomb here during WWII by scientists including Wu.

⬅ At the visitor centre you can learn more about the 'secret city' established here in 1943.

The Jurassic Coast

MARY ANNING

Lyme Regis, England

As a child, Mary Anning (1799-1847) was so poor she scoured the beaches around Lyme Regis for 'curiosities' to sell. Landslides in the cliffs exposed what she came to realise were fossils, and aged 12, she found the skull of an ichthyosaur. Over time, she became one of the world's most respected fossil hunters. She was not admitted to the Geological Society however, or always credited for her work. Finally, in 2010, 163 years after her death, the woman who inspired the tongue-twister, 'She sells seashells on the seashore' was declared one of the ten most influential British women in science by the Royal Society.

➡ Trains run from London Waterloo to Axminster with a connecting bus to Lyme Regis.

Barnard College

ANNIE NATHAN MEYER

Manhattan, USA

New York City's first private women's college came into being amidst widespread opposition. Its success may be mainly due to the spirited refusal of education activist Annie Nathan Meyer (1867–1951) to let the project die. Founded in 1889 as the women's division of Columbia and modelled on Radcliffe College, Barnard soon became a thriving hub of feminist ideology whose notable graduates include Margaret Mead, Zora Neale Hurston and Greta Gerwig.

A statue of Athena, the Barnard mascot, can be found close to a provocative bench by artist Jenny Holzer, eloquently conveying the college's balance of Ivy League tradition and progressive politics. Although Barnard students may now take classes at co-ed Columbia, it remains a haven for women to build bonds with one another.

⬅ To visit, take the 1 train uptown to 116th St.

USTA Billie Jean King National Tennis Center

BILLIE JEAN KING

Queens, USA

Winner of 39 Grand Slam titles, tennis great Billie Jean King is perhaps best known for her match against Bobby Riggs, billed 'the battle of the sexes' (and turned into a movie in 2017). Since retiring from tennis, she has continued to fight for equality off the court. Her influence is so vast that the prestigious annual US Open takes place at a tennis court named in her honour.

➡ Tickets usually go on sale at Ticketmaster in April or May but are hard to get for marquee games. General admission to early rounds is easier.

Great Rift Valley

BERYL MARKHAM

Nakuru, Kenya

Beryl Markham, an Indiana Jones character of the African bush, stood six feet tall, literally and in spirit. Born in England, she moved to present-day Kenya's Rift Valley with her divorced dad when she was four, and things got interesting. She hunted warthogs barefoot with spears, fell for horses and once got 'moderately eaten' by a lion. When her dad left to work in Peru, she stayed behind. At 17. No big deal. Beryl was just getting started.

She became Africa's first woman bush pilot and its first professional horse trainer (producing six Kenya Derby champs). She dated King George V's son and Denys Finch Hatton (played by Robert Redford in *Out of Africa*), and, notably, became the first solo pilot to cross the Atlantic east to west (landing safely, nearly out of fuel, in a Nova Scotia bog in 1936). Markham, who died in 1986 at age 83, summed up her experiences in her memoir, *West with the Night*, which Ernest Hemingway called 'a bloody wonderful book'. Famously, some critics doubted some woman bush pilot could write a book this good on her own. Beryl being Beryl, she just shrugged it off. As Paula McLain, whose novel *Circling the Sun* details Beryl's life, put it: 'she was too bold, too ambitious and too unwilling to be curbed by the constraints of her class or gender'.

📍 Visitors to Kenya's Rift Valley can stay in her childhood cottage, a lovely restored, century-old building with mountain views near Nakuru, in the landscape that she always came home to.

153

Shark Bay

ROSE DE FREYCINET

Gascoyne, Australia

In September 1818, shortly before her 24th birthday, Rose de Freycinet sat beside a teepee-like tent on the sandy coast of Shark Bay, about 25km (15 mi) north of today's Western Australian town of Denham, and announced that the oysters she had just tried were 'far tastier than all those I had eaten, sitting at a table in comfort, in Paris.'

In a watercolour and ink drawing of the occasion the adventurous young woman can be clearly seen, perched on a chair and reading a journal which may well be her famous diary. There's absolutely no sign of Ms de Freycinet in the official etching of the same scene, because her presence was totally unsanctioned and was scrupulously erased from the formal records. One of the first women to circumnavigate the world, she did so by stowing away on her husband Louis de Freycinet's expedition vessel *L'Uranie*.

Since it was never intended for official publication and eschews all the male preoccupations of exploration accounts, her diary is a unique record of the three-year trip around the world. It was only published in 1927 and not translated from French into English until 2003. Today that remarkable diary is a prize possession of the State Library in Sydney, a city where she stayed for five weeks and where, unofficial or not, she was the toast of the town. Although Sydney has changed vastly since then, wild Shark Bay still can bring to mind what Rose must have found on disembarking here.

🌿 Further afield, Rose Atoll in Samoa is named after de Freycinet.

© Andrea Izzotti / Shutterstock

© Pung / Shutterstock

Sabiha Gökçen International Airport

SABIHA GÖKÇEN

Istanbul, Turkey

Sabiha Gökçen (1913–2001) was a Turkish aviator who was the first woman in the country to receive a pilot's license. She's also believed to be the first female fighter pilot in the world. Adopted as a young orphan to be one of the wards of Mustafa Kemal Atatürk, Turkey's first president, her early exposure to Turkey's growing aviation industry ignited a lifelong passion, beginning with skydiver school and moving on to earn her pilot's license. Gökçen trained in military exercises and flew a combat mission in 1937. She became an aviation teacher in 1938 and trained other pilots until 1955.

State Library

PATSY MINK

Honolulu, USA

Highlights of Patsy Takemoto Mink's illustrious political career include co-authoring the groundbreaking Title IX Amendment of the Higher Education Act, still a major force in American education policy today, and introducing the Early Childhood Education Act. Born on Maui's north shore in 1927, she became the first woman of colour elected to the US Congress in 1964, serving 12 terms in the House of Representatives. Mink, a third generation Japanese American, also became the first Asian American woman to run for the presidential nomination, in 1972.

📍 Sabiha Gökçen International Airport in Istanbul, named after her, is located on the Asian side of the city, across the Bosphorus.

📍 Visit the bronze sculpture celebrating Mink's 'tireless advocacy' in front of Hawaii's State Library in Honolulu.

Johnson Space Center Memorial

SALLY RIDE

Houston, USA

While it took NASA 25 years to send the first woman to space, we couldn't have asked for a better role model than the woman they chose: Sally Ride. At just 32 years old in 1983, she made her first trip to space as part of STS-7 aboard the Space Shuttle *Challenger*. She flew again on *Challenger* for STS-41-G in 1984, and was training for her third mission when the *Challenger* disaster occurred in 1986. From that point on, Ride was earth-bound, and retired from NASA in 1987 to become a professor of physics. She served on the committees which investigated both the *Challenger* and *Columbia* accidents, and remained an active advocate for human spaceflight and women in STEM. After her death in 2012 it became public that she had spent most of her life partnered with Tam O'Shaughnessy, a professor emerita of psychology at San Diego State University. This makes her not only the first American woman in space, but the first LGBT astronaut.

Ride is memorialised with a small plaque in the memorial tree grove at Johnson Space Center in Houston, Texas, but note the grove isn't open to visitors except with a NASA employee escort.

If you can't visit Sally's tree in the grove, plan a trip to Space Center Houston, the official visitor centre for NASA Johnson Space Centre. You may even be able to have lunch with a current astronaut, many of them women.

Horagolla Bandaranaike Samadhi

SIRIMAVO BANDARANAIKE

Colombo, Sri Lanka

Sirima Ratwatte Dias Bandaranaike (1916–2000), known as Sirimavo, was originally a social worker. But shortly after her husband, Prime Minister SWRD Bandaranaike, was assassinated in 1960, she was herself elected prime minister of Ceylon (modern Sri Lanka), thus becoming the world's first non-hereditary female head of government. She would go on to serve two later terms (1970–77 and 1994–2000). Under her watch, which saw rising tensions with the Tamil people, the world had to start speaking of stateswomen as well as men (and perhaps learned they can err just as easily).

← You can visit Bandaranaike's family mausoleum at Horagolla Bandaranaike Samadhi, 38km (23 mi) northwest of Colombo.

Science Museum

ADA LOVELACE

London, England

History's first computer programmer and the only legitimate child of Lord Byron, Countess Lovelace (1815-1852) might not have been expected to be a mathematician by birth, but her mother promoted the young girl's studies in the sciences to balance her deceased father's flights of poetic fancy. In her work on Charles Babbage's so-called Analytical Engine, she published the first algorithm, and her notes reveal an early comprehension of computing's potential. STEM enthusiasts in her mold will love the Science Museum.

➡ For math geeks in particular, Mathematics: the Winton Gallery, designed by Zaha Hadid Architects, is a riveting exploration of maths in the real world.

Pennine Way

JASMIN PARIS

Edale, England to Kirk Yetholm, Scotland

The Spine race is a 431km (268 mi) ultramarathon along the Pennine Way each January. Runners have to carry all their equipment from start to finish. Given the non-stop nature of the race, sleeping is a tactical challenge: too much and you'll drop places, too little and you'll drop out. I entered the Spine in autumn 2018, when my daughter was 9 months old. I was struggling with motivation and needed something to aim towards. Running the Spine was an incredible and all-immersive experience. Racing the first day as a group, into strong wind and rain all day, and nearly getting blown over at Stoodley Pike. Running through the first night without sleep, and climbing Pen-y-ghent in the pink and gold dawn. Eating soup at Tan Hill Inn on the eve of the second night, before heading back into a long stretch of bogs, leading the race with Eugeni Roselló Solé. Three hours of glorious sleep at Middleton in Teesdale, then through the wet slippery rocks before Cauldron Snout, and up to the stunning vista of High Cup at dawn. Crossing the high point of the race at Cross Fell, before dropping to checkpoint 4, where I forged on alone. The exciting night that followed, racing to hold the gap along Hadrian's Wall and through the woods to Bellingham. Most of all, I remember the final day, crossing the remote Cheviot Hills, hallucinating for lack of sleep yet still aware of the beauty of my surroundings, my family waiting at the finish line. I'll treasure that memory for the rest of my life.

BY JASMIN PARIS

'Let things taste of what they are.'

Chez Panisse

ALICE WATERS

Berkeley, USA

Remember when the term 'farm-to-table' jumped into the cultural consciousness? When farmers markets suddenly popped up in every city across America? Or when organic food became something we all expected to see on the menu, rather than an eccentric exception? In the early 2010s restaurants across the United States and elsewhere began to proclaim their commitment to using local, organic ingredients, reducing the mileage between the producer and the plate. But these ideas were previously championed for decades by Alice Waters, who created fanatics about the local, organic, slow food movements through her own restaurant, Chez Panisse.

Waters opened Chez Panisse in 1971 in Berkeley, California. This was just a few years after Alice graduated with her degree in French Cultural Studies from nearby UC Berkeley, during which she had studied abroad in France. The chance to purchase local ingredients from her local market is one of the main sources Alice credits for her success; the ever-changing menu showcases the bounty of California in ways both creative and delicious, from sea scallops with watermelon radishes to wild nettle soup and trout rillettes.

In addition to Chez Panisse, still considered one of the best restaurants in the San Francisco Bay Area, Alice has advocated for healthy eating at home and better education around food science and nutrition. She established the Edible Schoolyard in 1995 to help teach organic gardening and cooking in schools starting in Berkeley; the Edible Schoolyard project since has expanded to schools in other major cities including Los Angeles, New Orleans, New York City and San Francisco. She also called for the Obamas to encourage organic farming and served as the inspiration for Michelle Obama's organic garden at the White House.

Reduce your carbon footprint during a visit to Chez Panisse by taking BART, one of San Francisco's public transit systems. It's a 15-minute walk from the Downtown Berkeley station to Chez Panisse. Reservations are recommended.

Federal Chancellery
ANGELA MERKEL
Berlin, Germany

'The question is not whether we are able to change but whether we are changing fast enough.'

Childhood pictures of Angela Merkel show her as an awkward kid with big eyes and a shy smile. Hard to fathom that this daughter of a Lutheran pastor, who grew up in socialist East Germany, would become one of the world's most powerful and respected political leaders. Some attribute her success as a politician to her analytical and pragmatic approach that had already served her well as a scientist (she holds a doctorate in quantum chemistry). When she vacates her office in Berlin's gleaming white Federal Chancellery in 2021, Merkel will have been Germany's first woman and first East German in the chancellor job as well as the longest-serving head of government in the European Union. During her tenure, which began in 2005, Germany grew into a beacon of stability and prosperity and Merkel became one of the EU's strongest leaders. Her fans call her 'Mutti' (Mommy), but Merkel's tenure has not been without controversy. Many in the EU regarded her handling of the Greek debt crisis negatively, while her open-door migration policy created criticism at home. But even most of her critics would admit that her role as a female trailblazer in German and global politics will reverberate through history for a long time to come.

Next door to the Chancellery is the famous Reichstag building, where a free lift whisks visitors to the rooftop for lovely views.

© H.W. Jargstorff / Shutterstock

Luskintyre Airfield
NANCY BIRD WALTON
Hunter Valley, Australia

Known as the 'Angel of the Outback', Nancy Bird Walton (1915-2009) earned her commercial pilot's licence at the age of 19, the first woman in Australia to do so. In 1935 she started flying for the Royal Far West Children's Health Scheme, acting as a flying ambulance to communities in remote parts of the outback, where she became a beloved figure and founded the Australian Women's Pilots Association. The new Sydney international airport, due to open in 2026, will be named after her, and Luskintyre Airfield has a memorial tower in her name.

← Nancy Bird Walton's ashes were scattered at the Luskintyre Airfield, and the garden there features Nancy Bird camellias.

Minnesota History Center
COYA KNUTSON
St Paul, USA

Coya Knutson, Minnesota's first female member of Congress, is a reminder of the potential as well as the waste of women's careers. After getting involved in local politics as an outlet from a violent marriage, in 1954 she ran as an independent for Congress and won. There she helped establish federal student loans and the school lunch program, but her success was cut short. Coya often returned to DC wearing big sunglasses to hide her bruised face, and her abusive husband published a letter called 'Coya Come Home' that urged Coya to quit politics and stay home with her 'loving' husband and son. Her career was ruined, but her legacy is still remembered in Minnesota – both her championing her community and her divorcing her no-good husband after his stunt.

→ At the Minnesota History Center, view the accordion Coya used to accompany herself while singing campaign songs.

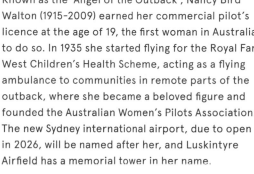

© Bettmann / Getty Images

> 'I have more brains, common sense and know-how generally than have any two engineers, civil or uncivil.'

Brooklyn Bridge

EMILY WARREN ROEBLING

Brooklyn, USA

When Emily married civil engineer Washington Roebling, her proclivity for science and math made them well-matched. In what history seems to suggest was a mutually agreed upon choice, Emily and Washington used their honeymoon as an opportunity to study caisson disease on behalf of Washington's father, who was designing the Brooklyn Bridge back home; it was an affliction many bridge workers suffered from. When Washington's father later died from tetanus as a result of work on the bridge, his son took over the project. Not long after, Washington was bedridden himself due to decompression sickness developed working on the underwater bridge footings.

For the remaining ten years of the project, Emily took over, quickly rising to the level of chief engineer in her own right. She was more than capable of handling the technical aspects of bridge construction as well as exceedingly adept at dealing with politicians, city managers, and bridge workers. Although neither Washington nor his father could be present at the bridge's opening, Emily well-deserved the honour of being the first person to cross the span. As a contemporary wrote, the landmark bridge is 'an everlasting monument to the sacrificing devotion of a woman and of her capacity for that higher education from which she has been too long disbarred'.

Stroll over the bridge from City Hall to DUMBO to enjoy Emily's accomplishment.

Allahabad High Court

CORNELIA SORABJI

Allahabad, India

If ever anyone wrote herself into the male-dominated ledgers of law, it was Cornelia Sorabji (1866-1954). She was the first woman to sit for Oxford University's Bachelor of Civil Laws in 1893. The first woman lawyer to appear before a court of the British Empire. The first woman to join the Allahabad High Court Bar in 1921. The 'old boys club' threw up wall after wall of difficulty: still, she rose, helping *purdanashins* (socially cloistered women) with their legal rights, then becoming legal advisor to the Indian government. Today, you'll find a Cornelia Sorabji Hall at the 1866-established Allahabad High Court; inaugurated in 1995, it is now a retiring room for woman advocates.

← You can only peer at the beautiful building of the Allahabad High Court from the outside, unless you're here for a trial.

National Track and Field Hall of Fame

WILMA RUDOLPH

Manhattan, USA

Wilma Rudolph was born one of 22 children on 23 June 1940 in Saint Bethlehem, Tennessee. Despite having polio as a child and being told she would never walk again, she became the fastest female runner on earth. At the 1960 summer Olympics in Rome she broke three world records while winning three gold medals: in the 100- and 200-metre individual events and the 4 x 100-metre relay. Upon returning to the US, she insisted she would only attend her victory parade if it was integrated. As she famously said, 'The triumph can't be had without the struggle'.

→ The National Track & Field Hall of Fame in Washington Heights' Armory is available for tours by appointment only.

Isabella Stewart Gardner Museum

ISABELLA STEWART GARDNER

Boston, USA

For most of history, it was rare enough for a woman to be listened to during her lifetime, but for her wishes to continue to be respected after her death? Who could ever achieve this except the sparkling Isabella Stewart Gardner (1840-1924). Following the death of her son and a miscarriage, Isabella fell into a deep depression. Luckily, the Gardners were very, very rich, and decided travel would lift Isabella's spirits. It did, inspiring her to become an educated and fearless collector of art.

Isabella told friends that, should she ever come in to her own money, she would use it to build a house full of art, open to anyone. When her father left her a giant sum, she did just that. Isabella's collection was the finest private collection in the world, with paintings by Titian, Vermeer and Rembrandt, plus objects from around the world that she used to build her iconoclastic museum. Once open, she regularly came down from her fourth floor apartments to personally arrange her collections for the public. Upon her death Gardner stipulated that nothing must ever be changed. In 1990 thieves made off with 13 priceless pieces. In accordance with her wishes that nothing be altered, the frames of the stolen art still stand empty on display in their galleries.

📍 Visitors with the name Isabella receive free lifetime admission at the museum.

Mount Everest Base Camp

GERLINDE KALTENBRUNNER

Khumbu, Nepal

Looming above its brethren in the Himalayas, Mt Everest remains the holy grail of mountaineers. Every May, hundreds of hopefuls gather at the tent city of Base Camp in Nepal, at the foot of the mountain, waiting for a window of favourable weather to make a push for the summit, and hardly a year passes without yet more climbers' lives being tragically claimed by Everest.

Nowadays, tour operators lead novices with deep pockets up the mountain, sometimes with disastrous results. There have been debates in mountaineering circles as to whether those who cannot summit under their own steam should be allowed on those hallowed grounds at all. There is no question, however, that Gerlinde Kaltenbrunner belongs up there: out of only nine people who have summited all fourteen 8000m peaks around the world without Sherpas, porters or supplementary oxygen, she is the only woman. She joined that small group of elite climbers after her difficult ascent of K2's North Pillar route in 2011, the culmination of years of effort.

As an Austrian growing up in Spital am Pyhrn, Kaltenbrunner climbed her first major peak when she was 13 years old and at the age of 23 she summited her first 8000m peak – Pakistan's Broad Peak. She funded her passion for climbing with her vocation as a nurse but became a professional mountaineer after bagging her fifth 8000m peak, Nanga Parbat. As someone whose life is permanently linked to the mountains, Kaltenbrunner has lost her share of close friends to mountaineering accidents and accepts the risk as part of her passionate pursuit.

'When a mountain beckons, how can I not go?'

♦ Even if you don't summit the mountain, hiking to Everest Base Camp is a tremendously beautiful, accessible trek (8 days up, 4 days down).

Herschel Museum of Astronomy

CAROLINE HERSCHEL

Bath, England

The eighth of 10 children born to a family in Hanover, Germany Caroline Herschel contracted typhus aged 10 and as a result never topped 4 foot 3 inches tall. 'She'll never marry', her family decided, and she became a Cinderella, labouring after her favoured older brothers.

So how did she become England's first salaried woman scientist and the first woman to be awarded a Gold Medal by the Royal Astronomical Society? Caroline had always been close to her brother William, and after he moved to England to pursue a successful career as a musician he persuaded his parents to let her join him as

his assistant. Music soon became a sideline to astronomy, and when he discovered the planet Uranus in 1781, he was instantly famous.

Caroline was an essential aide, recording his sightings while he remained glued to his telescope, and soon she was 'sweeping' the night sky in search of comets, a task she described as 'minding the heavens'. She discovered eight comets, and the comet 35P/Herschel-Rigollet bears her name. As does the C Herschel crater on the moon, while asteroid 281 Lucretia uses her middle name. She also discovered 14 nebulae and her catalogue of stars is still in use today.

📍 The Herschel Museum of Astronomy in Bath is in the Georgian House where Caroline and William lived and where they made their first discoveries.

© bento42894/Shutterstock; illustration © SSPL / Getty Images

Courtesy of NASA

NASA Katherine Johnson IV&V Facility

KATHERINE JOHNSON

Fairmont, USA

Imagine living to see your own life on the silver screen, your employer name a building after you, and receiving the Presidential Medal of Freedom. These are some of the recent highlights in Katherine Johnson's life; you'll recognise her name as the lead character in 2016's *Hidden Figures*, when she was played by Taraji P Henson.

Katherine Johnson was one of NASA's human 'computers' in the days before computer mainframes became commonplace. After humble beginnings from a blue collar family in West Virginia, Katherine became a stand-out math student and rose quickly to graduate high school at just 14 years old. She eventually joined the agency that would become NASA and worked on calculations for Mercury and Gemini astronauts, helping Alan Shepard become the first American in space and John Glenn complete the first orbit. Her calculations helped Apollo astronauts reach the moon and ensured the success of Space Shuttle missions; she even worked on an early proposal to send a mission to Mars.

In 2019 NASA honoured Johnson, who turned 101 that year, by naming the NASA Independent Verification & Validation Facility in West Virginia in her honour – just down the road from where Katherine worked on her graduate degree in mathematics from West Virginia University.

Check the Visit NASA site for information on where to explore the space program.

© Lukiyanova Natalia frenta / Shutterstock

'If we just fold our arms and yield, I would have no face to see our ancestors after death. If we must perish, why not fight to the death?'

Summer Palace

EMPRESS CIXI

Beijing, China

The walkways of Beijing's sprawling Summer Palace have been trodden by many pairs of imperial feet, including those of Empress Dowager Cixi (1835–1908). Today, Cixi is remembered with a mixture of respect and distaste. Having risen to a position of influence as a favoured concubine of the Xianfeng Emperor, Cixi helped plot a coup after his death. She secured rule through her infant son and consolidated her power by assuming regency and ignoring traditional rules of succession.

The most powerful and long-lasting dowager empress in China's history, it was under her orders that the Summer Palace was refurbished in 1888, after damage from the Second Opium War. In the Hall of Joy and Longevity, Cixi kept her living quarters. The Tower of Buddhist Incense is where she made offerings and prayed for favour. The Hall of Dispelling Clouds is where Cixi entertained guests and hosted rituals and grand celebrations. Cixi also kept enemies under house arrest here, confining the Guangxu Emperor to the luxuriant surrounds of the Hall of Jade Billows. Cixi also famously ordered restoration of the decorative 'marble boat' in 1893, using funds that had been earmarked for the navy, a move seized upon as a symbol of hollow decadence. Cixi's shrewd pursuit of power and talent for self-preservation have created an image of her as a schemer, but some historians see her as savvy rather than ruthless, focused on keeping control of the empire.

📍 Take subway line 4 to Beigongmen to arrive within a five-minute walk of the Summer Palace's North Gate.

Guggenheim Museum

PEGGY GUGGENHEIM

Venice, Italy

Few art aficionados have a life so deeply intertwined with the art and artists that they collect as Peggy Guggenheim (1898-1979) did. The younger generation of the celebrated financial family, Peggy Guggenheim sought to set her life apart, throwing her passion and influence into the art world from the very start. Raised in New York, she joined the art scene in Paris in the 1920s and mixed with the likes of Marcel Duchamp and Constantin Brâncusi. Her artistic predilections ran the gamut from cubism and surrealism to abstract expressionism well before they were popular. And her NYC-based gallery, Art of the Century, was created in the eye of the art it was selling — with the surrealist section full of curving lines and the cubist section adorned with blue canvas walls and art on pulleys. She would go on to champion the work of Jackson Pollock, Mark Rothko and Robert Motherwell, among many others. In 1948 Guggenheim brought her vast collection to the Venice Biennale, and a short time later bought the 18th-century Palazzo Venier dei Leoni on the Grand Canal. With a long, low façade and verdant gardens, the palazzo would become not just her home but the home of her celebrated collection and the museum that we know today.

📍 The Guggenheim Museum is one of the most visited sights in Venice — book your ticket ahead of time.

JÓHANNA SIGURÐARDÓTTIR

þingvellir National Park and Reykjavik, Iceland

Jóhanna Sigurðardóttir, Iceland's prime minister from 2009 to 2013, thereby became the first openly gay head of state in the world (and head of the world's oldest parliament). She had been active in labour unions and became a member of parliament in 1978 with an avowed liberal and social justice agenda. As prime minister she saw the nation through the aftermath of the enormous financial meltdown that occurred in 2008. She married her partner in 2010 on the very day that same-sex marriages were legalised in Iceland.

⬅ Iceland's parliament, the Alþingi, was created at þingvellir in AD 930; the modern Alþingi moved into Reykjavík in 1881.

Fanny Blankers-Koenlaan

FANNY BLANKERS-KOEN

Amstelveen, Netherlands

Dutch athlete and hero Fanny Blankers-Koen was nicknamed 'The Flying Housewife' due to her stellar performance at the 1948 Olympics in London. A star of track and field, excelling in the sprints, hurdles and high jump, she won four gold medals in London — the most ever won by a single female athlete. She accomplished this amazing feat, in fact, while pregnant! Over the course of her magnificent career, Blankers-Koen set 16 world records in eight different events. In 1999 the International Amateur Athletic Federation named her the 20th century's top female athlete.

➡ Visit a statue of Fanny mid-stride on Van Aerssenlaan street in Rotterdam. A street in Amstelveen also bears her name.

Fanny Blankers-Koenlaan
Atlete 4 gouden medailles Londen 1948

The University of Al Quaraouiyine

FATIMA AL-FIHRI

Fez, Morocco

If you've ever wondered how universities first came about, the answer may surprise you. It's all thanks to pioneering Muslim woman Fatima al-Fihri, who founded the world's first university along the twisting medieval alleyways of Fez in 859. While much of her story is lost in time, it's known that she emigrated to Morocco's spiritual and cultural capital from Kairouan (present-day Tunisia) with her merchant father and younger sister Mariam.

Devout and well-educated, after her father died she chose to spend her inheritance on building a mosque and a hub of learning that would benefit her adopted city, naming it Quaraouiyine after her birthplace. At first it only offered religious instruction, but the syllabus gradually broadened to include mathematics, science, law, philosophy, astronomy and the Arabic language. Open to scholars of all ages and religions, it created academic and cultural bonds between Europe and the Islamic world.

August alumni include the Muslim historian Ibn Khaldun, the Jewish philosopher Maimonides and the future Pope Sylvester II. Much later, Fatima al-Kabbaj, one of the university's first female students who graduated in the mid-1950s, became the first woman on Morocco's Supreme Council of Religious Knowledge.

Expanded over successive dynasties until it became one of the largest mosques in Africa, today's sprawling complex isn't open to non-Muslims, but you can often get a glimpse of its courtyard – resplendent with dazzling *zellij* (mosaic tilework), elaborately carved stucco and ornate cedar wood – through the open doorway. Fittingly, a female Fassi architect, Aziza Chaouni, was tasked with restoring the university's historic library in 2012, though the job isn't yet finished. It's the world's oldest working library, and accordingly one filled with precious manuscripts and priceless ancient tomes, including a 9th-century Qur'an.

Fatima's vision and commitment not only created what is officially the world's oldest existing, continually operating higher-educational institution but it paved the way for universities around the globe, including the first in Europe, founded in Bologna in 1088, and Harvard in 1636.

© Wondervendy / Shutterstock

© saiko3p / Shutterstock

📍 The entrance to the mosque is on Derb Boutouil; wander down the Talaa Kebira and you'll stumble across it, though only practising Muslims may enter.

Apia Harbour

ZITA MARTEL

Upolu, Samoa

In the year 2000 a local church on Upolu, Samoa, needed a skipper for their *fautasi* (longboat) racing boat, which can be crewed by as many as 50 rowers. They knew Zita Martel had rowed in college, and yeah, she was a woman and no woman had ever been part of a fautasi team before, but she was their best option. At first Zita declined but eventually she agreed and history was made.

Martel led her team to win after win, including against the faster fibreglass boats from American Samoa and in the championship held on the year of Samoa's 50th independence anniversary – which also happened to be the year of Zita's 50th birthday. She attributes part of her team's success to her motherly love that helps bond the team together as one.

In 2013 the first all-woman fautasi crew hit the waters, continuing the cultural change that Zita began. That same year Zita, no one-trick pony, also brought home a gold medal in archery at the South Pacific Games. She celebrated where life had taken her by getting *malu*, traditional Samoan leg tattoos, using the painful comb and mallet technique. This 'Queen of the Longboats' has since used her local fame and strong voice to speak out against domestic violence in the country.

The major fautasi races of the year take place in Apia Harbour over the Teuila and Independence Festivals.

Liaquat Bagh

BENAZIR BHUTTO

Rawalpindi, Pakistan

On the one hand, Liaquat Bagh is just a sun-scorched park in Rawalpindi. On the other, its rolling green has been blighted by memories of massacre. Pakistan's first Prime Minister was assassinated here in 1951, after whom the park was subsequently named; dozens of Awami National Party workers were killed on the same spot in 1973, supposedly at Bhutto's father's behest; and lastly it saw the assassination of Benazir Bhutto herself, twice prime minister from 1988 to 1990 and 1993 to 1996, and the first woman to be elected as head of government in a Muslim country.

When Bhutto first swept to power in 1988, she was a glamorous 35-year-old with Oxford and Harvard degrees, and all the power of her people behind her. She was the first woman to have a child while in office, way back in 1990. 'The next day I was back on the job, reading government papers and signing government files', she later wrote. It wasn't to last. Charges of corruption weighed heavily; she was accused of illegally amassing a fortune for herself. Then, just before re-election in 2007, Bhutto was assassinated by the Pakistani Taliban here on the green of Liaquat Bagh.

Take a taxi or the local Rawalpindi-Islamabad Metro Bus service to get there, though there is no memorial on site.

© Robert Nickelsberg / Getty Images

Tower of the Moon and the Stars

QUEEN SEONDEOK

Gyeongju, South Korea

Make a journey to the ancient capital of the Silla Kingdom in Gyeongju to visit the Tower of the Moon and the Stars, or Cheomseongdae, the oldest observatory found in Asia today. Built around AD 632 during the reign of Korea's first female monarch, Queen Seondeok, it's said that the astronomers who used the tower had to lie on their backs to watch the stars through the roof! Queen Seondeok, known for her intelligence and ability to bridge ties during a tumultuous period in Korean history, wasn't only interested in astronomy though – legend has it that she was so perceptive, she could even interpret signs and predict events. One legend states that Queen Seondeok was able to predict an attack from a rival kingdom after hearing the croaking of frogs by the pond and so, was able to successfully capture the invading soldiers. As a child, she was chosen as heir due to her intelligence – she was able to tell a peony had no scent by an illustration of the flower with no insects around it!

Queen Seondeok was an insightful leader, and by strengthening ties with China later enabled the Silla to gain victory over the other kingdoms in Korea. The observatory she built was the first of its kind and inspired other observatories in Japan and China. Cheomseongdae is built with 27 levels, to match the queen's role as the 27th ruler of the Silla Kingdom. The roof of this 9m-tall (30ft-tall) tower forms the shape of the Chinese character for 'well'. At a time when women were not necessarily powerful, Queen Seondeok led the way in astronomy and politics, inspiring female rulers and scientists in generations to come.

 The Tower of the Moon and the Stars is located in a wildflower-filled park complex on the southern edge of the city.

Utrecht University

ANNA MARIA VAN SCHURMAN

Utrecht, Netherlands

Anna Maria van Schurman (1607–1678) was the first woman to attend university in Europe. Unusually for her time, her parents gave her the same education that they gave their sons, and when her prodigious intellect became obvious, they allowed her to continue learning rather than switch to domestic arts. A true scholar, she attended Utrecht University and became a writer, artist, philosopher and theologian. She spoke at least 14 languages – from French to Turkish, Arabic and Ethiopian. Van Schurman was also a visual artist, and she wrote poetry in Dutch, German, Greek, Latin and Hebrew. Renaissance woman would be both an understatement...and a truth.

Her endless accomplishments led van Schurman to be considered the most learned woman in Europe, and she both corresponded with and was visited by many learned men and women of the European intelligentsia and upper classes, from royalty to writers and mathematicians. She advocated for higher education for women in her book *The Learned Maid*. Certainly her own life amply showed that women were suited to pursuits of learning, if only they could be allowed latitude to pursue the same opportunities as men rather than be prepared for matrimony only.

📍 You can visit Utrecht University, where Anna Maria van Schurman studied, and near where she lived for the bulk of her life.

Canossa Castle

MATILDA OF TUSCANY

Canossa, Italy

Matilda of Tuscany (1046–1115) was one of the most powerful figures of the Italian Middle Ages. Her dominion covered a vast swath of Northern Italy, including Modena, Reggio, Mantua, Ferrara and Tuscany. Her father, Boniface II of Canossa, was a Lombard noble and her mother, Beatrice, was the niece of Emperor Conrad II. After the death of her father and two older siblings, young Matilda became the heir to their great holdings. A devout Christian, Matilda supported the papacy in its struggle against the Holy Roman Emperor, a conflict now known as the Investiture Controversy.

Matilda's life was filled with adventures, from being held hostage with her mother by Emperor Henry III to donning armour to fight in battles against Henry IV. She gave immense support to her close friend Pope Gregory VII, and it was at her castle in Canossa that Henry IV bent a knee to the Pope. Matilda's personal life was relatively drama-filled as well, with two marriages, including one to 17-year-old Welf V, Duke of Bavaria and Carinthia, when she was 43. Unusually for her era, Matilda was a broadly educated intellectual, who spoke many languages and was a powerful arts patron.

📍 Visit Matilda's seat of power in the Apennine Reggiano hills at the ruins of Canossa Castle, which now also houses a museum.

© Nostalgia for Infinity / Shutterstock

Baikonur Cosmodrome

VALENTINA TERESHKOVA

Baikonur, Kazakhstan

In remote western Kazakhstan (part of the Soviet Union until 1991), lies Baikonur Cosmodrome, an odd patch of land that's officially Russian soil – until 2050, at least, when the lease runs out. The site of the launch of the first man into space in 1961, in 1963 Baikonur made history once more when the Vostok 6 space capsule launched under the command of 26-year-old Valentina Tereshkova, first woman in space. She spent over 70 hours in space, making 48 orbits of our planet before landing in the Altai mountains.

Tereshkova didn't have experience as a pilot when she volunteered for the Soviet space program, but she was chosen because of her extreme hobby. She'd racked up 126 parachute jumps for the Yaroslavl Air Sports Club, and at the time, astronauts were required to parachute from their capsules seconds before they hit the ground. Valentina never flew in space again, but she did become a test pilot and instructor and was honoured with the title of Hero of the Soviet Union.

Baikonur may only be visited as part of a guided tour; arrange well in advance.

Indira Gandhi Memorial Museum

INDIRA GANDHI

New Delhi, India

Indira Gandhi's whole life was striped with violence. In her 18 years as India's Prime Minister (she was elected to the post four times), she saw the fracturing of Bangladesh from Pakistan, navigating an 11-month war with the latter (India won). Her son died in an airplane crash. Her work was riven by charges of corruption. She blanketed the country under emergency rule, stampeding over Constitutional rights, and sweeping dissidents into jail. Perhaps worst of all, her tenure saw horrific state-sponsored violence against the Sikh community, monstrous retribution for a brief rebellion by Sikh terrorists in Punjab. She died the same way, murdered in 1984 by Sikh bodyguards haunted by her betrayal. Several years later, her other son (quickly named prime minister after her assassination) was blown up by a suicide bomber. But you won't see too much of this at her home, now converted into the Indira Gandhi Memorial Museum. What you will find instead are books, piles upon tottering piles, plenty of photographs, elegant, tasteful furniture, even the last sari she ever wore. It's a poignant reminder of a powerful woman once known as the only man in her cabinet.

📍 The museum's closest metro station is Lok Kalyan Marg.

© Kriangkrai Thitimakorn / Shutterstock

The Beehive

JACINDA ARDERN

Wellington, New Zealand

New Zealand's Jacinda Ardern took office in 2017 at the age of 37 – while pregnant. Despite her youth she is not the youngest Kiwi prime minister. Nor is she the first female PM (she's the third), though that is not surprising as New Zealand led the way in suffrage by granting women the vote in 1893, the first democratic nation to do so. Yet Jacinda's prime ministership has been trailblazing on many fronts: her savvy social media; raising her daughter to speak both te reo Māori as well as English; and her compassionate response to the Christchurch mosques shooting. Ardern's decision to refuse to give the perpetrator any notoriety and her unifying actions as she comforted the victims, modelled a new and powerful response to acts of terror. All concurrent with Prime Minister Ardern starting her family while leading the country.

The place where this formidable leader has wowed the world with her speeches (and amused them with her part in the Rhys Darby comedic Tourism New Zealand advertisement dubbed #getNZonthemap) is New Zealand's parliament in its capital, Wellington. Next to the neoclassical parliament buildings is the Beehive, a modernist building and home to the government's executive wing and the prime minister's offices. Free daily tours of New Zealand's parliament start here from the ground floor visitor centre.

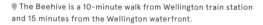
The Beehive is a 10-minute walk from Wellington train station and 15 minutes from the Wellington waterfront.

© Robert CHG / Shutterstock

© John Moore / Getty Images

Executive Mansion

ELLEN JOHNSON SIRLEAF

Monrovia, Liberia

'The size of your dreams must always exceed your current capacity to achieve them. If your dreams don't scare you, they are not big enough.'

Ellen Johnson Sirleaf, the first African female head of state, was born in 1938 Monrovia to an indigenous Gola father and a German mother. After earning a master's degree from Harvard University, Madam Sirleaf returned to Liberia and served in the ministry of finance under President William Tolbert and in President Samuel Doe's military dictatorship. She gained publicity during this time for her financial integrity, clashing with both heads of state. She was sent to prison twice during the Doe regime and given a 10-year prison sentence after she criticised the military government in the 1985 national elections, when

she contested a seat in the senate. After a period in exile and a failed presidential run in 1997, she finally was elected president of Liberia, serving from January 2006 until January 2018.

Her tenure saw a growing economy, the Ebola epidemic and accusations of nepotism, but the country was at peace during her 12 years in office. Sirleaf was one of the recipients of the 2011 Nobel Peace Prize for her efforts to further women's rights, and was awarded the 2017 Ibrahim Prize for Achievement in African Leadership, recognised for Liberia's peaceful transition of power and recovery after the country's long period of civil unrest.

📍 The Executive Mansion is closed to the public, though admirers of Sirleaf's tenure can visit her bust in the Garden of Nations on Costa Rica's University of Peace campus.

Ocean Village Marina

TRACY EDWARDS

Southampton, England

When skipper Tracy Edwards and her 12 crewmates navigated a second-hand yacht named *Maiden* out of Ocean Village Marina in 1989, they were sailing into history as the first-ever all-female team in the Whitbread Round the World Race (now called the Volvo Ocean Race), the sport's toughest competition. The boat carried the weight of widespread criticism and sexism; one reporter even described *Maiden*, which Edwards and her team refurbished themselves, as a 'tin full of tarts'. Nine months and nearly 33,000 nautical miles later, Edwards, then 27, and her crew had defied naysayers in triumphant fashion, sailing back into

Southampton to a second-place finish in their division. Edwards earned an MBE honour and the Yachtsman of the Year Trophy, the first time it was awarded to a woman. Thirty years later *Maiden's* remarkable story made its big-screen debut in an eponymous documentary. Meanwhile, *Maiden* is sailing once again, following years of neglect in the Seychelles after a post-Whitbread sale. In 2014 Edwards heard about her plight and jumped into action to buy and restore her, launching a two-year world tour aboard *Maiden* to raise funds and awareness for girls' education and empowerment initiatives – with an all-female crew.

◆ Well-known as the starting/finishing point for round-the-world yacht races, Southampton's Ocean Village Marina is a charming waterfront area brimming with shops, bars and restaurants.

Topkapı Palace Harem

ROXELANA

Istanbul, Turkey

Sultans ruled the palaces in the male-dominated Ottoman Empire, but Roxelana (1502-1558) proved the old adage that behind every great man is a great woman. The great man in this case was Süleyman the Magnificent, whose 16th-century reign was the highpoint of the Ottoman Empire's 600-year rule. Roxelana's rise from the harem through the imperial ranks reads like a *Game of Thrones* storyline, beginning with her humble childhood in present-day Ukraine. Kidnapped at 15 by Crimean Tatars, she was taken to Constantinople (Istanbul), finding her way to the Topkapı Palace harem as a gift to Sultan Süleyman from the all-powerful Valide Sultan (sultan's mother). She outshone her many rivals, most significantly the mother of Süleyman's heir, and became the Haseki Sultan (chief consort), earning the nickname *Hürrem,* akin to cheerful in Persian.

It does seem more than coincidental that several obstacles to Roxelana's meteoric rise met a grisly end. İbrahim Paşa, Süleyman's old friend and devoted grand vizier, was strangled for objecting to her influence, while the presumed heir Mustafa was also executed, ensuring Roxelana's children's survival and the succession of her oldest son. This may seem a trifle Machiavellian to modern sensibilities, but remember that royal fratricide was commonplace to the Ottomans; Ahmet I, that big softie, later replaced it with the 'cage life' tradition of keeping siblings under house arrest.

Certainly, Roxelana broke the mould and gained an unprecedented level of power, ushering in a 150-year period known as the Sultanate of Women, when the Haseki Sultans and Valide Sultans wielded great political influence. Roxelana broke ground by having a hand in Süleyman's policies at a time when the empire reached its territorial and cultural zenith, and the mosques, madrasahs, hammams and soup kitchens she commissioned can still be seen from Istanbul to Mecca. For a privileged look at the sequestered world she entered and conquered, tour the chambers and courtyards of the 300-room harem at the Ottoman sultanate's Topkapı Palace.

Topkapı Palace is in Sultanahmet (Istanbul Old City), entered through the Imperial Gate next to the Aya Sofya (Hagia Sophia).

© Dietmar Rauscher / Shutterstock

Harry's Bar

JAN MORRIS

Venice, Italy

Jan Morris turned 92 in 2018, meaning she had been Jan for as long as she had been James. Possibly the most remarkable of her books is *Conundrum*, an account of the operation she underwent in Casablanca in 1972. Gender reassignment was not so common in those days and James was also required to divorce his wife Elizabeth as part of the process. James may have departed, but Jan and Elizabeth continued their lives together and once same-sex marriage was permitted they remarried in 2008. Their gravestone is waiting under the stairs of their home in Wales: 'Here are two friends, at the end of one life.'

Morris will be best remembered for secretly conveying the news back from the Everest Base Camp – runners and telegrams, there were no satphones in those days – that the mountain had been climbed. The 1953 news arrived in London simultaneously with Queen Elizabeth's coronation. The Morris literary collection ranges from Australia (*Sydney*) to England (*Oxford*), right across the USA (*Coast to Coast*) or all around the British Empire (*The Pax Britannica Trilogy*), but none of her books is better known than her 1960 love letter to Italy's most iconic city: Venice. And where better to encounter Jan Morris in Venice than her old haunt Harry's Bar, where the 18-year-old British soldier ventured through the canalside doors in 1945.

Harry's Bar is the originator of the peach bellini, and also serves a classic gin-heavy dry martini (no olive).

Cheung Chau Windsurfing Centre

LEE LAI-SHAN

Hong Kong, China

Windsurfer Lee Lai-shan may not be a household name worldwide, but in Hong Kong she's a treasured daughter. She won gold for the city in the 1996 Atlanta Olympics – the only Hong Konger to ever do so. Lee grew up on the island of Cheung Chau, just six miles from frenetic central Hong Kong but spiritually on a different planet. Its small harbour bobs with fishing boats, laundry hanging from their masts like flags. The main village echoes with the melodic ding of bicycle bells as residents cycle past each other – there are no cars allowed here. Its narrow lanes are lined with seafood restaurants, incense-fragrant temples and shops selling local snacks. Across a narrow isthmus is the main beach, whose velvety sands are thronged with day trippers each weekend. To the right, across a small headland, is quieter Kwun Yam Beach. This is Lee's territory. She trained here at the Cheung Chau Windsurfing Centre, run by her uncle. The laid-back spot offers windsurfing classes and equipment rentals – go for a spin on the blue-green South China Sea, then chill with a beer at the little outdoor café. Then visit one of the island's four temples dedicated to Tin Hau, goddess of the sea. In this ocean-circled city, women who rule the water get the respect.

📍 Cheung Chau is a 35-minute ferry ride from Hong Kong's Central Ferry Piers.

Château de Chenonceau

CATHERINE DE' MEDICI

Loire Valley, France

Few women in history were mightier than Catherine de' Medici (1519-1589). Born in Florence to Italy's formidable Medici clan, she wielded her power in France as queen consort of Henry II (whom she married at the age of 14) and later as regent of France. Her sparkling personality was the sensation of the French court. She gave birth to 10 children, seven of whom survived. Her political influence was particularly strong during the French Wars of Religion between the Catholics and the Huguenots. When Henry II died in a jousting accident, she was catapulted further onto the political stage. Though their eldest son Francis was made king, he died after less than a year. Their second son, Charles, was only ten years old when he became king in 1560, so Catherine acted as regent, ruling the country. Even when her next son, Henry III, succeeded Charles after his death, de' Medici wielded enormous power, wrangling continuously, though without success, to bridge the sides in the ongoing civil wars.

One of the sorrows of Catherine de' Medici's life was the dedication of her husband to his mistress Diane de Poitiers. He gave de Poitiers the castle at Chenonceau, one of the most elegant in the Loire Valley. De Poitiers designed its distinctive arches and a formal garden. After Henry's death, Catherine de' Medici forced de Poitiers to exchange it for the less grand château of Chaumont and completed Chenonceau's construction herself.

📍The architectural fantasy land of Chenonceau is largely the work of several remarkable women, hence its alternative name, *Le Château des Dames*: 'Ladies' Château'.

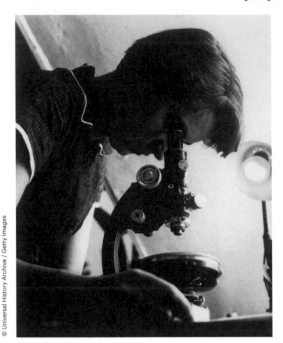

© Universal History Archive / Getty Images

Donovan Court, Drayton Gardens

ROSALIND FRANKLIN

London, England

Crick, Watson and Wilkins famously shared the Nobel Prize for their discovery of the DNA double helix, and for many years nothing was said to acknowledge the contributions of their fellow scientist, Cambridge-educated Rosalind Franklin (1920-1958), to our understanding of its molecular composition. But while her research in understanding the nature of DNA strands was overlooked until after her death, posthumous recognition finally arrived. Today, a blue plaque adorns Franklin's one-time London home in honour of her studies of molecular structure.

◀ Rosalind Franklin lived at Chelsea's Donovan Court until her death at 37 of ovarian cancer in 1958.

Golden Gate Bridge

KIM CHAMBERS

San Francisco, USA

From the frigid North Channel to the shark-infested waves of the Pacific Ocean, there isn't a body of open water on the planet Kim Chambers hasn't dreamed about swimming. And we're not talking about a casual dip: Chambers, a native New Zealander, is one of the world's most successful long-distance swimmers. In 2014 she became just the sixth person (and third woman) ever to complete the Oceans Seven Challenge, the gruelling swimming equivalent of the Seven Summits mountaineering challenge. She continued swimming into the record books, in 2015 becoming the first woman to swim solo from the Farallon Islands to the Golden Gate Bridge, completing the feat in 17 hours, 12 minutes.

© franckreporter / Getty Images

➡ On a clear day, you can spot the Farallon Islands from the Golden Gate Bridge and several other viewpoints.

The Golden Threshold
SAROJINI NAIDU
Hyderabad, India

Just past the jammed, cacophonous streets of the Abids neighbourhood stands a bone-white bungalow with an arcaded balcony, teetering at the edge of the University of Hyderabad. This is the Golden Threshold. Today a cultural hub hosting plays, talks and readings, once it was the home of Sarojini Naidu (1879-1949), her four children, her husband and her clutch of pets. But who was she? School literature textbooks in India are strewn with poems by Naidu, a fellow of the Royal Society of Literature and the 'Nightingale of India', as she was popularly known (*The Golden Threshold* was the name of her first book).

But to merely classify Naidu as a poet would be to flatten her achievements. For she was also the first Indian woman to be President of the Indian National Congress in 1925, a time when the country was struggling to throw off the yoke of the British (who imprisoned her three times). Oh, and there's also the small matter of her becoming governor of the United Provinces (now Uttar Pradesh), from 1947 to her death in 1949.

📍 Hyderabad's main attraction for visitors is the ornate Charminar mosque (pictured below).

Qián Tomb
WU ZETIAN
Xi'an, China

China's sole female emperor, Wu Zetian (AD 625–705) succeeded her husband Emperor Gaozong in the culmination of a journey that began when the young girl became the concubine to his father, Emperor Taizang. From there, she ruthlessly acquired power in her own hands until decision-making effectively rested with her alone. She would use her position, among other things, to elevate Buddhism's role over Taoism and Confucianism. The long spirit way to her impressive tomb is lined with enormous, lichen-encrusted sculptures of animals and officers of the imperial guard, culminating with 61 (now headless) statues of leaders of ethnic groups in China who attended the emperor's funeral. Two stelae on the ground each stand high here: The Wordless Stele (Wúzi Bēi) is a blank tablet, and one story relates how it symbolises Empress Wu's absolute power, which she considered inexpressible in words. She is buried here with her husband Emperor Gaozong, whom she succeeded, China's lone Empress (as opposed to a Dowager Empress).

Tour bus 2 runs close to here from Xī'ān train station and returns in the late afternoon.

National Aviation Hall of Fame

BESSIE COLEMAN

Dayton, USA

Decades before Queen Bey wowed audiences, another woman of colour set the bar high – sky high, in fact. Though she was born to share-croppers before the turn of the 20th century and was consistently barred from pursuing her dreams, Bessie Coleman – or 'Queen Bess' to airshow attendees – rose above every obstacle put before her. An excellent student who lacked the financial resources to pursue higher education, she set out for Chicago in 1916. There she met Robert Abbott, publisher of the *Chicago Defender*, who helped publicise her dream to become the first African American and Native American woman pilot. While American aviation schools consistently rejected

her based on race and gender, Queen Bess set sail for France, where she did indeed become the first woman of both African American and Native American descent to earn an international pilot's license in 1921.

Back in the US, Coleman excelled at airshows in the days before commercial flights were common. She pushed beyond the boundaries for her race, gender and class and dreamed of opening an aviation school for African American pilots. Unfortunately, an aircraft accident in 1926 cut that dream short. Eighty years after her untimely death, she was at last inducted into the National Aviation Hall of Fame.

📍 The National Aviation Hall of Fame is located on Wright-Patterson Air Force Base near Dayton, Ohio. Next door, you can also visit the National Museum of the Air Force, and the Huffman Prairie Flying Field Interpretive Center is just off-base, where the Wright Brothers made early flight attempts.

'Like billowing clouds, like the incessant gurgle of the brook, the longing of the spirit can never be stilled.'

Hildegard of Bingen Trail

HILDEGARD OF BINGEN

Bingen am Rheim, Germany

Mention the name Hildegard of Bingen (1098-1179) today and you might get an indifferent shrug or a confused frown. Hildegard who? Back in 12th-century Germany, however, Hildegard was quite the medieval A-lister, and is still held in reverence in holistic healing and religious circles some 900 years later. Born around 1098 to a noble family in the Rhineland, Hildegard had visions as a child, claiming to see the light of God through five senses, and was raised as an anchoress in the Disibodenberg monastery from the age of eight. She went on to found two abbeys of Benedictine nuns, as well as being a healer, mystic, writer, composer of lyric poems and songs, naturalist and linguist. She penned revolutionary books on diet and herbal cures, natural history, theology and medicine that drew on ancient Greek humourism, some of which are still read for their insight and relevance to this day. She was, in a nutshell, pretty darned talented. One of the great early protofeminists, strong-willed Hildegard exercised a firm belief in equality and was always ready to stand up to her male counterparts. She went on preaching tours that called for people to rebuke the abuse of power, injustice and corruption in the church. In other words, she was a spiritual, medical and eco warrior way ahead of her time.

Thankfully we are catching up, and in 2012 Hildegard was canonised as a saint. Saints, of course, attract pilgrims, which is where this 6.7km (4 mi) circular footpath along the romantic, castle-dotted Rhine Gorge slots into the picture. Setting off from Rüdesheim, the trail affords spirit-lifting views over the vine-ribboned banks of the river, providing insights into Hildegard's life en route to the Benedictine Abbey of St Hildegard, where she stands immortalised in bronze, dressed in habit, eyes closed as if in prayer. Come in the contemplative calm of morning or evening to feel the spirit of this special soul, as the hairs-on-end sound of lauds and vespers drift from the abbey just as they did in the 1100s.

The trail begins at the landing stage of the Bingen/Rüdesheim passenger ferry or at Rüdesheim railway station.

'Can you persuade people to take your side when you're not sure in the end you'll be there to take theirs?'

British Cemetery

GERTRUDE BELL

Baghdad, Iraq

Born in 1868 to a wealthy British family, Gertrude Bell might well have lived her whole life in England in a traditional women's role. Instead, she began travelling at 24, scaling the Alps and eventually becoming one of the most influential people in the Middle East through her work as a writer, archaeologist and political administrator. Bell built up extensive networks of contacts and gained respect in the region, and was instrumental in the formation of the countries of Jordan and Iraq. She began to be known as *Al Khatoun*, 'The Lady', and is considered as important in Iraq's early history as more well-known TE Lawrence – though later chroniclers would focus on him to her exclusion.

In the 1920s Bell organised Iraqi elections, helped place King Faisal in a constitutional monarchy and acted as director of the new Antiquities Museum. Upon her death she was buried in the British Cemetery in Baghdad, which remains one of the few remaining testaments to the decades of British intervention in Iraq. You can still visit her stone tomb there, or opt against a trip in favour of viewing the documentary about her legacy, *Letters from Baghdad*.

The British Cemetery, sometimes called the British Army Cemetery or Baghdad North Gate War Cemetery, is a seven-minute drive from the Baghdad Central Railway Station across the Tigris River.

Baffin Island

MATTY MCNAIR & SARAH MCNAIR-LANDRY

Nunavut, Canada

Dressed in an orange parka, snow pants, and sturdy boots, Sarah McNair-Landry looks like any athletic woman you might encounter on a ski run or hiking trail. But McNair-Landry and her mother Matty McNair are modern-day Arctic adventurers, based on Baffin Island in Canada's Nunavut territory. Matty McNair, who guided the first all-woman expedition to the North Pole in 1997, also led Sarah and her brother Eric on a 2003 South Pole trip that made them the youngest people to reach that landmark. McNair-Landry later retraced the entire length of the Northwest Passage on kite skis and circumnavigated Baffin Island by dog sled, recreating a trip her parents made 25 years earlier.

The McNairs founded Iqaluit-based outfitter Northwinds Expeditions, where McNair-Landry now leads Arctic expeditions, offers extreme polar training and guides regular travellers on dog-sledding and kite-skiing adventures. It's not all about the fun of exploring, either: the family raises awareness of climate change as well as countering stereotypes about what an explorer looks like.

📍 Getting to Baffin Island (shown below) requires dedication. First Air flies non-stop to Iqaluit from Ottawa and from Montreal via Kuujjuaq.

© Manuel Lacoste / Shutterstock

Maria Skłodowska-Curie Museum

MARIE CURIE

Warsaw, Poland

Lining Freta Street in Warsaw are frescoed
houses in tasteful shades of ochre, mustard and
rose-pink. The occasional baroque church spire
rises above the cobblestones. It's a view that
double Nobel Prize-winning scientist Marie Curie
(1867–1934) would recognise: born and educated
in Warsaw, Curie spent a year of her young life
living on Freta Street, where a museum now stands
honouring her achievements.

While the world remembers her as Marie
Curie, the Maria Skłodowska-Curie Museum is
so named because Curie never entirely dropped
her maiden surname, as she was fiercely proud
of her Polish identity. Poles are just as proud
of her: the physicist and chemist made an
incalculable contribution to developing the theory
of radioactivity. Discovering a rare radioactive
element, she named it polonium to draw attention
to the plight of Poland, which was under partition
at the time.

The Maria Skłodowska-Curie Museum, in a
finely restored 18th-century building, presents
documents and scientific apparatus from Curie's
life and work, including photographs with her
husband Pierre Curie – with whom she shares
one of her Nobel prizes. It's fascinating to see
the documents and equipment presented here,
though it's sobering to note that they cost Curie
her life: she died at 66 from an autoimmune
disease brought on by the harmful effects of
repeated exposure to radiation.

📍 The museum is a 10-minute walk northwest of Warsaw's Stare
Miasto bus and tram stop.

© Eye Ubiquitous / Getty Images

Sydney Olympic Park

CATHY FREEMAN

Sydney, Australia

Winning gold for Australia at the Sydney 2000 Olympics in the 400m sprint, Cathy Freeman brought Australians together in a way no one else could by carrying both the Aussie and Aboriginal flags on her victory lap around the stadium.

At the time, Australia was strained by racial tensions. The country had been rocked by the findings of the 1997 Bringing Them Home report on the Stolen Generations, inquiring into Indigenous children forcibly removed from their families. Meanwhile, just a few months before the Olympics, 300,000 people had walked across the Sydney Harbour Bridge in support of reconciliation and a national apology to the Stolen Generations, the largest Australian political demonstration ever.

'It was always a dream of mine to not only win an Olympic gold medal but to do the victory lap with both flags...I hold the Aboriginal community in such a high place in my heart so I'm very proud of my Indigenous roots.'

Freeman's victory thrilled the nation and her victory lap became a symbolic act of reconciliation that held enormous power. The track where 110,000 spectators watched her cross the finish line metres ahead of her closest rivals (and where she lit the Olympic flame) is at Sydney Olympic Park, and today you can visit sculpture-studded Cathy Freeman Park on the grounds. In 2007 she established the Cathy Freeman Foundation to support Indigenous education. Born in Queensland, Freeman remains the sixth-fastest woman of all time.

Sydney Olympic Park continues to host a plethora of concerts and events on its grounds.

Massachusetts Institute of Technology

MARGARET HAMILTON

Cambridge, USA

While it's impossible to deny that Neil Armstrong and Buzz Aldrin's first steps on the moon were historic, it's also important to understand how much prepatory work was done by the 400,000 people who made it possible. These people include Margaret Hamilton, whose computer engineering work on the Apollo Guidance Computer laid the groundwork for Armstrong and Aldrin to land on the lunar surface in the first place. Hamilton was the head of a team that helped develop the computer software for the Apollo and Skylab missions.

As a young woman in a predominantly male field, Hamilton's computer prowess was undeniable, and the list of her areas of expertise is so long that it's hard to imagine what she wasn't an expert in. After working with NASA she went on to start her own software company and is credited with having come up with the name 'software engineering' to describe the work she and her colleagues did.

📍 MIT is just off the Kendall T stop on Boston's public transport system. MIT grounds are open to the public and you can pick up a self-guided walking tour map at the Events and Information Center on campus.

© Elijah Lovkoff / Shutterstock

National Cowgirl Hall of Fame

ANNIE OAKLEY

Fort Worth, USA

There can be few more macho professions on Earth than the cowboy: for even one cowgirl to carve a name for herself in this rough, tough male world is remarkable. Yet exhibition shooter Annie Oakley (1860-1926) did so and more, as fans of the musical based on her life, *Annie Get Your Gun*, will be aware. Born in a log cabin, Annie took to shooting to be able to provide for her family in rural Ohio before taking her talents out on the road. Take a trip to Texas' National Cowgirl Hall of Fame to pay her and her ilk homage.

Fort Worth styles itself as the place 'where the west begins' due to its position on the 19th-century cattle ranching run, Chisholm Trail, and the National Cowgirl Hall of Fame here is more accurately a tribute to the pioneering women of the American West. Cowgirls, rodeo champions and sharpshooters are heralded, as well as the women who have excelled at preserving the culture of the American West, from country and western singers to artists to writers (other women honoured include cowgirl Faye Blessing and country and western singer Patsy Cline). Annie Oakley, of course, can hold her own against all comers. Highlights include the design-your-own horse, western shirt and boots installation, and the holographic representation of Oakley having a chat with you about her life.

Interested in seeing a modern day cattle drive? The Fort Worth Herd parades in Stockyards National Historic District twice daily.

Royal Palace

QUEEN CHRISTINA

Stockholm, Sweden

Queen Christina of Sweden (1626–1689) lived an eccentric and eventful life. Her father, Gustav II, expecting great things from her, instructed that the girl be raised as a prince. He then promptly went off and died in the Battle of Lützen, leaving his six-year-old successor and his country in the hands of the powerful Chancellor Oxenstierna.

Christina received a boy's education, becoming fluent in six languages and skilled in the art of war, and she took her oath as king, not queen, earning her the nickname 'Girl King'. Spats with Oxenstierna increased as she grew older. After being crowned queen in 1644, she often defied him. In 1649 Christina made public her desire not to marry, and abdicated in 1654. Disguised as a man, she rode through Denmark on horseback, as tense relations between the two countries would not have allowed her true self safe passage. Christina ended up in Rome, where she converted to Catholicism – a scandalous act at the time. She is one of only four women to be buried in the basilica of St Peter's in Rome.

A strong woman known for her bisexuality, in modern times Christina has become a lesbian icon, while her cross-dressing has made her a favourite of the transgender community.

Stockholm's Royal Palace replaced the Tre Kronor Castle of Christina's time, located in the same spot, which burned down in 1697.

10

FEMALE PIRATES
and their
FAVOURITE HAUNTS

Think piracy is reserved for men only? Think again. These ten women sailed the world's waters, plundering on a legendary scale. Avast ye!

1 ANNE BONNY Nassau, the Bahamas

This legend of piracy's Golden Age menaced the Caribbean with her lover Calico Jack in the early 1700s, when Nassau was the capital of the 'Republic of Pirates'.

2 CHING SHIH Macau, China

After her pirate husband died in 1807, Ching Shih expanded his Red Flag Fleet into the bane of the China Seas. She died a free – and rich – old woman at home in Macau.

3 SAYYIDA AL-HURRA Tétouan, Morocco

This 16th-century Islamic pirate queen (and ally of Barbarossa) ruled the ancient Moroccan port city of Tétouan as governor before terrorising the Mediterranean to avenge the Muslims who'd been run out of Spain by the Inquisition.

4 SADIE FARRELL New York, USA

Known as 'Sadie the Goat' (and claimed by some to be an apocryphal figure), Sadie is said to have roamed the New York waterfront of the 1860s as part of the Charlton Street Gang of river pirates all along the Hudson River.

5 MARY READ Spanish Town, Jamaica

Disguised as 'Mark', Mary fought in the British army before hightailing it to the Caribbean to join Calico Jack and Anne Bonny in piracy's Golden Age.

6 JEANNE DE CLISSON Brittany, France

When her husband was executed for treason, the 14th-century 'Lioness of Brittany' bought three warships and sailed the English Channel looking for French ships to attack as revenge.

7 INGELA GATHENHIELM Gothenburg, Sweden

Piracy as...statescraft? With royal permission, Gathenhielm and her husband plundered the ships of Sweden's enemies in the early 1700s. They're buried together in sarcophagi carved with the Jolly Roger.

8 PRINCESS SELA Norway

The scourge of the 5th-century North Atlantic, this Viking pirate princess was described as being a 'skilled warrior and experienced in roving'.

9 ANNE DIEU-LE-VEUT Tortuga

Deported to Tortuga from France, Dieu-Le-Veut married a notorious Dutch pirate (he fell in love after she threatened to shoot him) and took to the seas.

10 RACHEL WALL New England, USA

Rachel Wall, born in Pennsylvania circa 1760 and hanged in Boston in 1789, took a 'maiden in distress' route to her pirating; after storms, she feigned needing assistance on the *Essex* until ships came to her rescue. Once they did, their vessels would be robbed by Rachel and her crew.

ICONS

Westminster Pier

BOADICEA AND HER DAUGHTERS

London, England

Pedestrians stream across Westminster Bridge, cameras at the ready. Here's Big Ben and the Palace of Westminster to the left, the London Eye slowly turning across the river. There's so much to see that many visitors don't even stop and take a selfie with the statue, impressive though it is, this bronze goddess in her chariot, spear in hand.

Meet Boadicea, the Celtic queen who revolted against the Romans. When her husband died in 60 AD, he left his holdings to his two daughters and the Roman emperor Nero. But the Romans annexed his lands, flogged Boadicea and raped their daughters. Boadicea vowed revenge. She raised an army of her fellow Iceni tribespeople and laid waste to the cities of Londinium (London), Camulodunum (Colchester) and Verulamium (St Albans), killing as many as 80,000 Romans and Roman sympathisers. When the revolt failed, she allegedly drank poison.

According to the Roman historian Tacitus, Boadicea led her people into battle with these words: 'Consider how many of you are fighting – and why! Then you will win this battle, or perish. That is what I, a woman, plan to do! – let the men live in slavery if they will'.

Thomas Thornycroft's statue of brave Boadicea and her daughters was erected in the reign of Queen Victoria, a symbol of patriotic heroism and, ironically, of Britain's imperial ambitions.

'Rome shall perish - write that word
In the blood that she has spilt.'
—William Cowper, *Boadicea: An Ode*

The statue is on the northeast corner of Westminster Bridge.

> '**I'm willing to buy a horse and saddle, To go to battle in my father's place.**'

Mulan Temple

HUA MULAN

Yingguo Village, China

Everyone knows how the legend goes. Hua Mulan, according to the 6th-century *Ballad of Mulan*, was just a girl from central China who took her aging father's place in battle disguised as a man, with no one the wiser. Trained in martial arts, sword fighting and archery, she fought alongside the men for twelve years. At the end of her time in the army, she was offered a high-ranking post, but turned it down to return to her family. Because this story is part of an oral tradition, no one knows if she actually existed. Some give the tale a sadder ending that explains the lack of historical record: that Mulan, in protest against the emperor's wishes, killed herself. With several conflicting tales, there's quite the mystery surrounding Mulan.

Was she a real person? Was she a member of the Tuoba people who ruled during the Northern Wei period, and were more closely related to the Turkic or Mongol people? Regardless, the stories surrounding Mulan represent feminism, filial piety and strength, which may be why her tale is so long-lasting. This legend now spans across the globe, inspiring young women that they too can do whatever men can. Go back to her origins to check out her purported hometown of Yingguo Village in today's Henan province where the Mulan Temple, built during the Tang Dynasty, honours her life and courage. Two steles in front of the temple, dating from 1334 and 1806, record the saga of Mulan, one which shows no signs of fading.

Located 35 km (22 mi) south of Yucheng county seat, Mulan Temple can be found at the end of Jiangjun Rd, just west of the middle school.

Longstone Lighthouse

GRACE DARLING

Farne Islands, England

The treacherous reefs off the Northumberland coastline have long been a seafaring hazard: not only is the ocean around rough but at least five isles are regularly concealed by tides. Dramatic-looking red-and-white-striped Longstone Lighthouse was the fifth attempt to establish a beacon on the Farnes sufficiently communicating surrounding perils to ships. The ride out to this lighthouse-cum-visitor-centre on the outermost skerry of the archipelago can be choppy enough in a motorised vessel today. But it was significantly more savage on a stormy morning in 1838 when the *Forfarshire*, carrying 62 souls, foundered on rocks here and the only means of rescuing them was by an even more exposed and vulnerable rowboat.

Grace Darling (1815-1842), daughter of lighthouse-keeper William Darling, spied the wreck and survivors. With weather too inclement for the lifeboat to launch from the mainland, she and her father rowed out the longer, more sheltered way around the rocks to reach those stranded in a tempestuous sea. The Darlings saved nine of those on board and father and daughter were awarded medals for their bravery. But Grace, as a woman who had distinguished herself in a man's world, and a good-looking one at that, became a national inspiration. Gifts were showered upon her from afar; even marriage proposals were made. Her fame outlasted her; Grace died of tuberculosis four years later.

Boat trips leave from Seahouses, Northumberland. Only one operator, Golden Gate, is licensed to land at Longstone.

© Andrew Balcombe / Shutterstock

Truganini Lookout, Bruny Island

TRUGANINI

Tasmania, Australia

A Palawa woman from the first-contact generation, Truganini (1812–1876) grew up in her traditional culture on Bruny Island, Tasmania. At this time there were six times as many white men as white women in the colony, and many settlers engaged in violence and rape against Aboriginal women and children. This violence is one of the key triggers historians cite for the Black War which raged in Tasmania between 1824 and 1831.

A casualty of the times, Truganini's mother, uncle and fiancé were all killed by settlers, her sisters, Lowhenunhue and Maggerleede, were enslaved by sealers, and she herself was raped. Yet despite her traumas, during 1830–35 Truganini acted as an ambassador for her people when she travelled with George Augustus Robinson and assisted his efforts to broker peace. She later went with him to Victoria but there joined a group of Indigenous guerrilla fighters and was implicated in the murder of settlers. At last she and the other surviving Aboriginals were forcibly moved into a settlement camp.

Truganini plays a symbolic role in Australian history, as she's been painted as the melancholy 'last of her race' and then reclaimed as a strong and defiant symbol of survival for the Tasmanian Aboriginal community. Before her death in 1876 Truganini asked to have her ashes scattered in D'Entrecasteaux Channel, yet the Royal Society of Tasmania displayed her skeleton at Hobart's Tasmanian Museum. Finally in 1976 her wishes were honoured with cremation, and museums around the world are slowly repatriating similar remains. It's one small consolation that her legacy has led to revisiting the practices she opposed.

Near her birthplace on Bruny Island, you can visit the Truganini Lookout to experience something of her ancestral land.

Knocknarea
QUEEN MEDB
Sligo, Ireland

Medb was a woman who knew what she wanted – power, sex and revenge – and she got them all. She ruled as queen of the province of Connacht for 60 years, took an impressive amount of lovers and lived to see her children kill her rapist first husband. Her desire to always be exactly as wealthy as her fourth husband sparked a war between Connacht and Ulster that is the epicentre of the Irish epic *Táin Bó Cúailnge*. Her rather undignified ending (she was killed with a piece of cheese thrown by a sling) is made up by her impressive reputed burial place in a cairn on the summit of Knocknarea with magnificent views of Sligo Bay. A short, steep hike will get you to the summit to where she is said to be buried upright, spear in hand, looking towards the north to be ready for the return of her old enemy, the army of Ulster. Said to have lived around 50 BC, it's unclear whether she was a legend, reality or a mix between the two but her legacy remains throughout the west of Ireland with plenty of places named after her.

📍 From Strandhill, follow the signs for Knocknarea which will bring you to the car park. From there, the cairn is an hour's ascent on a clear trail. Do not remove any stones from the cairn.

Taj Mahal

MUMTAZ MAHAL

Agra, India

Many are those who have admired the monumental Taj Mahal: Poet Rabindranath Tagore described it as 'a teardrop on the cheek of eternity'; Rudyard Kipling as 'the embodiment of all things pure'; while its creator, Emperor Shah Jahan, said it made 'the sun and the moon shed tears from their eyes'. Yet not all know its origin story as one of the most elaborate tombs in existence. The Taj was built by Shah Jahan as a memorial for his third wife, Mumtaz Mahal, who died giving birth to their 14th child in 1631. The death of Mumtaz left the emperor so heartbroken that his hair is said to have turned grey virtually overnight. Construction of the Taj began the following year; although the main building is thought to have been built in eight years, the whole complex was not completed until 1653. Not long after it was finished, Shah Jahan was overthrown by his son Aurangzeb and imprisoned in Agra Fort, where for the rest of his days he could only gaze out at his creation through a window. Following his death in 1666, Shah Jahan was buried here alongside his beloved Mumtaz.

 Remember to retrieve your free 500ml bottle of water and shoe covers (included in Taj ticket price).

© Elera Ermakova / Shutterstock

'I demanded more rights for women because I know what women had to put up with.'

Casa Rosada

EVA PERÓN

Buenos Aires, Argentina

Raised in poverty but ascending to become Argentina's first lady, a campaigner against all social injustices and more popular than the president himself, Eva Perón (1919-1952), better-known as Evita, remains to this day an iconic champion of the common people, throughout Argentina and far beyond.

She married Juan Perón just prior to him becoming president of Argentina in 1946, but his success in the polls was often because of none other than his wife. Evita became increasingly influential within Perón's party. Young, beautiful and from a humble background, she was a big hit with the working class. She founded the Eva Perón Foundation, Argentina's largest charitable organisation, which funded everything from shoes to new schools and homes for the needy.

She campaigned for women's suffrage and labour rights. Eventually she determined she would run for Vice-President, a position she would likely have attained to judge from her standing amongst the masses. Only deteriorating health and opposition from the political elite stopped Evita's ascendancy, as she died tragically of an aggressive cervical cancer in 1952.

Of the many locales associated with Evita, the salmon-pink Casa Rosada, ornate residence of Argentina's president, is most iconic. Eva often addressed her thousands of supporters from the balcony, and made her last public speech – appropriately delivered on Loyalty Day, commemorating the huge demonstration she organised for Juan Perón's 1945 release from prison – in 1951.

Casa Rosada abuts Buenos Aires' Plaza de Mayo, where crowds famously thronged to hear Evita speak.

© Cedric Weber / Shutterstock

Compton Tennis Courts

WILLIAMS SISTERS

Compton, USA

Born in Michigan, from a young age the Williams sisters, winners of multiple Grand Slams, lived in the neglected district of Compton in Los Angeles, moving to South Florida when the sisters were 9 and 10 so that they could attend a tennis academy. Nearly every day in their earlier childhood, their father would take them and a bucket of tennis balls to two basic public Compton courts ringed by fences, and teach them the formidable serving,

volleying and rallying skills that later conquered the world of women's tennis. The area itself, immortalised in *Straight Outta Compton*, has achieved fame thanks to music stars Dr Dre, NWA and Kendrick Lamar. As for the Williams sisters, their athleticism and tenacity is now a sport legend, and the courts they once practised on have been refurbished and dedicated to them as the Venus & Serena Williams Court of Champions.

The Martin Luther King Transit Center in Compton is the best transit hub to visit the tennis courts.

Le Cordon Bleu

JULIA CHILD

Paris, France

There's cooking school and then there's Le Cordon Bleu. Its graduates staff the kitchens of elite restaurants and hotels from Salzburg to Singapore, scooping quenelles of crème fraiche, chiffonading parsley, folding fish en papillote. It also does a brisk business in people who go on to become TV chefs – Mary Berry, Ming Tsai and Giada De Laurentiis among them. And then, of course, there's the queen of them all, the person who made being a TV chef into a thing: Julia Child.

Child was in her late 30s when she attended the Paris institution. She had already graduated from Smith College, been a working girl in 1930s New York, and joined the OSS (a predecessor of the CIA) during WWII before famously having her taste buds awakened by a meal of sole meunière in Rouen. She'd go on to become the most famous French cook in America, parodied on SNL, portrayed on film by Meryl Streep, her kitchen enshrined in the Smithsonian Institute. If French cooking sparks your own sense of joie de vivre, then you too can attend Le Cordon Bleu in homage to Child. You don't need knife skills or a six-month leave of absence to take one of their standalone classes. Although the school was founded in 1895, the ultramodern flagship campus opened in 2016.

Le Cordon Bleu's Paris campus is at 13-15 Quai André Citroën.

'I have done things according to the design of my heart.'

Mortuary Temple of Hatshepsut

HATSHEPSUT

Luxor, Egypt

The temple of Hatshepsut stands on the Nile's west bank, framed by sun-scoured cliffs. It's a fittingly timeless monument to Hatshepsut (1508–1458 BC), the first woman to obtain the full powers of the pharaoh title. Hatshepsut became regent after the death of her husband, Thutmose II. Taboos of the era meant the pharaoh role was considered male but Hatshepsut's royal blood – she was the wife, daughter and sister of a pharaoh – strengthened her case when she demanded full coronation. Hatshepsut's time as pharaoh was characterised by peace and prosperity; her two decades of rule were a boom time for construction and trade.

To immortalise her rise to power, Hatshepsut commanded that the story of a woman pharaoh's birth be carved into the walls of her mortuary temple. To ancient Egyptians, the afterlife was as vivid as life itself. Consequently the duty of constructing a fitting monument was a lifelong endeavour. Hatshepsut modelled her own on the temple of monarch Mentuhotep II...but insisted it be built on a much grander scale. In Hatshepsut's day, landscaped gardens and frankincense trees would have granted welcome shade. Today, visitors feel the full force of desert heat as they approach the temple. It was common for pharaohs to chisel away the achievements of their predecessors; after her death, carvings honouring Hatshepsut were smoothed out of the temple walls on the orders of her stepson. Nonetheless, it has been impossible for history to forget her.

📍 Hatshepsut's Memorial Temple, also called Djeser-Djeseru. is 8km (5 miles) northwest of Luxor Temple; get a taxi.

© Stitchik / Getty Images

Moomin World

TOVE JANSSON

Naantali, Finland

Swedish-speaking Finnish author and artist Tove Jansson may be best known for creating her beloved Moomin books for children, for which she was awarded the Hans Christian Andersen Award, but she's also a queer icon. She and her lifelong partner visited each other by way of a secret passage between their houses in Helsinki, and spent summers retreating to their own island. So it's fitting that the charming amusement park celebrating her creations, Moomin World, is housed on its own island across the bridge from Naantali's Old Town. The focus is on hands-on activities and exploration, not rides.

← Fans can also visit the Moomin Museum in Tampere, further north of Naantali's Moomin World.

Rani Abbakka Study Centre

ABBAKKA CHOWTA

Bantwal, India

Queen Abbakka Chowta is known as the first Indian woman to revolt against European colonialism, in 1555. She firmly repulsed the Portuguese whose mighty flotilla of galleons tried to overwhelm her patch of the Indian Ocean in Karnataka (it used to be a haven for traders from Egypt, Persia and Arabia), sending out boats that brought down two Portuguese warships with flaming arrows. Yet her extraordinary story, which earned her the name *Abbhaya Rani* (fearless Queen), would have been written out of history except for Professor Thukaram Poojary. He put together a museum, the Rani Abbakka Tuluva Adhyayana Kendra, with thousands of artefacts relating to her life.

→ The Rani Abbakka Study Centre is about an hour's drive from Mangalore Airport; it is closed on Tuesdays.

Dollywood
DOLLY PARTON
Pigeon Forge, USA

'If you don't like the road you're walking, start paving another one.'

Dollywood is a self-created ode to the patron saint of East Tennessee: the big-haired, big-bosomed and big-hearted country singer Dolly Parton. One of 12 children born into a one-room log cabin, her father paid the doctor who delivered her with a bag of cornmeal. Yet with a talent for singing and songwriting, she made it to Nashville after graduating high school, and went on to become one of the most successful country stars ever. Along the way she has been helped by a strong head for business, famously refusing to give up half ownership on her song 'I Will Always Love You' in return for Elvis Presley covering it. Instead

Whitney Houston came along decades later and provided a new interpretation for the ages. Eager to give back, she built Dollywood to create local jobs; Parton also created the Imagination Library to donate books to children for early literacy, with over 105 million books donated as of 2018. She's also garnered a strong LGBT following for her open and accepting attitude. A fun and friendly place, her park features Appalachian-themed rides and attractions, a water park, mountain crafts and more. As a child, Dolly Parton let her imagination run wild, and now, visitors to her theme park in the hills of the Smokies can reap the benefits.

Want to get to know the singer's catalogue? Her first album, 1967's *Hello, I'm Dolly* is as good a place to start as any.

'Power without a nation's confidence is nothing.'

Catherine Palace

CATHERINE THE GREAT

St Petersburg, Russia

The rise of Catherine the Great (1729–1796) ushered in a golden age for Russia. After helping to engineer a coup against her husband, Peter III, Catherine soon secured power. During her long reign as Catherine II she not only expanded the empire but effected widespread cultural changes: pioneering educational reform, championing the arts and improving women's access to centres of learning. Countless buildings bear the imprint of Catherine's talent for classical design, including the Hermitage, Russia's largest repository of art. But the best place to trace the empress's footsteps is Catherine Palace in Tsarskoe Selo.

Catherine Palace was actually named for a preceding Catherine: Peter the Great's second wife, Catherine I, who reigned for three years and commissioned the palace as a summer residence. Decades later, Catherine the Great applied her more understated aesthetic to the palace (and halted plans to cover its statues in gold). Though badly damaged during WWII, the palace has been marvellously restored: the ornate rococo building is resplendent in powder blue and gold. Catherine was the target of salacious gossip and some of her political moves are remembered with bitterness: for instance, the empress carved up Poland after a failed uprising in 1794. The face Catherine wanted to show to the world is displayed in the palace's Portrait Room, where visitors file in to meet the gaze of the regally attired empress.

📍 Catherine Palace is at the Tsarskoe Selo estate, outside of St Petersburg. Check the (limited) opening hours ahead of your visit.

Historial Jeanne d'Arc

JOAN OF ARC

Rouen, France

'I do not fear men-at-arms; my way has been made plain before me.'

Few early feminists create such fascination as Joan of Arc (Jeanne d'Arc in French), often depicted on horseback in her banner-waving, battle-going armour. Born into a peasant family in 1412 Domrémy-la-Pucelle, the so-called 'Maid of Orléans' has, over the past six centuries, been held up as visionary saint and a feverish fanatic, a heroine and a heretic sinner.

She could have stayed at home spinning wool by her mother's side, but instead, undeterred by her illiteracy and spurred on by visions of saints and the voice of God, Joan seized what she believed was her divine destiny - to help Charles VII lead France to victory in the Hundred Years' War with England. Victorious she was, until finally the Burgundians, a group of nobles allied with the English, captured her in 1430. She was later tried for witchcraft, heresy and cross-dressing, found guilty and burned at the stake on the central square in Rouen in 1431, aged just 19.

Where the story of Joan ends, Rouen's insightful, interactive museum picks up. Set in the highly atmospheric vaults of the archbishop's palace, the immersive museum evocatively brings to life Joan's rise and fall, shedding light on the lady behind the legend and the famous trial.

📍 The museum is located right in the medieval heart of Rouen, just steps from the mighty Gothic Cathédrale Notre-Dame.

© jorisvo / Shutterstock

© Amlan Mathur / Shutterstock

Ahilya Fort

AHILYABAI HOLKAR

Maheshwar, India

Queen Ahilyabai Holkar ruled here from 1765 to circa 1796, building a maze of residences, offices and audience hall within the fort. Her 30 year reign was exceptional – few enemy armies nipping at her heels, no fractious political intrigues, no tides of miserable subjects bent under the weight of heavy taxes. Instead, she built roads, wells, tanks, rest houses and temples, promoting artisans and spurring on the tradition of the local textile industry. Her kingdom was a cradle of peace and prosperity. Which brings us to the second part of her legacy; the recent resumption of textile weaving by Ahilyabai Holkar's descendants. The indomitable Sally Holkar's Rehwa Society and Women Weave have single-handedly revived the flagging Maheshwari handloom industry, providing employment for plenty of weavers, and offering free education to their children.

📍 Ahilya Fort is a half-hour drive off the Mumbai-Agra Highway. Book a night's stay at ahilyafort.com. The Queen's heirs have transformed her crumbling residence in Ahilya Fort into a charming boutique hotel.

'There are still so many causes worth sacrificing for. There is still so much history yet to be made.'

Mayfair Academy of Fine Arts

MICHELLE OBAMA

Chicago, USA

Michelle Obama, lawyer and university administrator, best-selling author, and the first African American first lady of the United States, started out as another local girl in south Chicago. Growing up she enrolled in dance classes at local institution Mayfair, a family-owned performing arts academy founded by famed tap dancer and choreographer Tommy Sutton. There she imbibed pride in her heritage and learned about the joy of community ties. No wonder that today when Michelle Obama discusses her own story, the city of Chicago is a major character. When Barack Obama was elected to the presidency in 2008, the family kept their Hyde Park home and their South Side roots in the city. This Chicago neighbourhood known for its diversity, urban authenticity and beauty made the perfect home base. While the Obama girls took their own dance classes and went to school in DC, their mother was balancing work and life in her historic role.

Throughout her journey, Michelle Obama's commitment to community has mirrored the values of Chicago pillars like Mayfair, still thriving under the careful eye of Peggy Sutton, Tommy's daughter and another woman who knows the importance of making young black girls see the beauty in themselves. In the White House, Michelle spearheaded initiatives for public health, targeting childhood obesity and encouraging healthy lifestyles through activities like dance. While she represents the South Side by way of birthright, today she inspires the entire city and beyond to embrace their authentic selves and to move with the confidence and poise of a South Side dancer.

📍 Mayfair still offers dance classes in all genres for kids and adults. Also on the South Side is the former first lady's childhood home at 7436 S Euclid Ave and her elementary school, Bouchet International School, 7355 S Jeffery Blvd.

Kelders 33
MATA HARI
Leeuwarden, Netherlands

'A courtesan, I admit it. A spy, never! I have always lived for love and pleasure.'

Dutch exotic dancer and femme fatale Margaretha MacLeod (1876–1917) is better known to the world as Mata Hari. She had a troubled youth and first marriage with an abusive husband, after which she went on her own to Paris. Harnessing her good looks and her new knowledge of Indonesian dances acquired in the Dutch colonies, in 1905 she debuted on stage as Mata Hari (a Malay expression meaning sunrise), an exotic dancer. Mata Hari wore skimpy bejeweled costumes and charmed crowds with sensuously danced tales of dramatic passion.

During WWI, Mata Hari was recruited by the Germans to spy for their war efforts, but despite taking a fortune in payment, she ultimately refused the offer. Later Mata Hari did, however, spy for the French. When they intercepted a communique suggesting she was actually spying for the Germans as well, the French promptly executed Mata Hari by firing squad. It is still not known definitively whether she was, indeed, a double agent for the Germans. Her scandalous reputation may have made her ripe for disbelieving.

📍 Mata Hari was born in Leeuwarden and the statue of her there depicts her mid-dance.

Clare Island

GRÁINNE NÍ MHÁILLE

County Mayo, Ireland

Also known by her anglicised name, Grace O'Malley (1530–1603), Ireland's Pirate Queen made her living raiding coastal towns, islands and passing vessels, setting sail with a group of loyal warriors from her home castle of Clare Island, a large rocky outpost standing guard in Clew Bay. Upon her father's death, she took over the lordship, becoming wealthy, independent and notorious. According to one legend, she gave birth to her fourth child on one of her ships, then rose from her bed the next day to successfully defend an attack. Her fame made her a target of the English governor, who took her family into captivity. As a result, Gráinne appealed to Queen Elizabeth I and won a remarkable personal meeting with her in 1593. Despite her refusing to acknowledge Elizabeth as queen of Ireland, they did strike an accord, but Gráinne soon went back to supporting Irish insurgents and is said to have remained on the seas until her death at the age of 73. Her resting place is believed to be the O'Malley tomb in the Clare Island Abbey on the southern part of the island; the church itself was built by her ancestors and still stands today.

📍 A ferry runs to Clare Island daily from Roonagh Pier, outside the town of Westport. There is accommodation on the island if you want to extend your stay.

'Love of country is deep-seated in the breast of every Hawaiian, whatever his station.'

Iolani Palace

QUEEN LILI'UOKALANI

Honolulu, USA

The story of Iolani Palace, the only royal residence on United States soil, is forever linked to the life of Hawaii's last monarch, Queen Lili'uokalani (1838–1917). The tale of this imposing Honolulu manor begins first with Lili'uokalani's brother and sister-in-law. In the late 1800s, when the kingdom of Hawaii was an independent nation that maintained diplomatic relations with more than 80 countries, Hawaii's King Kalakaua and Queen Kapiolani built Iolani Palace as their royal residence.

Completed in 1882, the ornate stone palace was a mix of Hawaiian influences and the era's prevailing European style, outfitted with the first electric lights in Honolulu. The mansion's grand staircase was crafted from local wood, while its furnishings were shipped from a furniture maker in Boston. The king commissioned a San Francisco artist to etch hula dancers onto crystal panels for the doors to the main salon. Unfortunately, since the artist had never seen this traditional Hawaiian dance, the doors instead feature Greek performers. When King Kalakaua died in 1891, his sister succeeded him, becoming known as Queen Lili'uokalani and taking up residence in Iolani Palace. Born Lydia Kamakaeha, the queen was also a songwriter; her best-known composition may be, 'Aloha Oe (Farewell To Thee)', which became something of an island anthem. The new queen's reign was short, however; she was deposed in a US-led coup in 1893 (remember, this was long before Hawaii became part of the United States). Lili'uokalani was placed under house arrest and imprisoned in Iolani Palace. In the chamber where she was confined, a quilt she made remains on display, embroidered with the dates when she was born, ascended to the throne and was overthrown and imprisoned. No other place evokes a more poignant sense of Hawaii's history.

📍 Today, you can learn about the palace and the queen's history on informative guided tours, offered Tuesday through Saturday, or explore on your own with a self-guided audio tour.

Sultanahmet Square

EMPRESS THEODORA

Istanbul, Turkey

Empress Theodora (circa AD 500–548), the most powerful woman in the history of the Byzantine Empire, had a life that was not short on drama. Born in poverty on the fringes of the Byzantine Empire, she became an actress, a scandalous pursuit at that time that was synonymous with prostitution. Ambitious, intelligent, and shrewd from the start, she moved to Alexandria, Egypt, at 16 and converted to Christianity, renouncing her former lifestyle. Not long after she met the heir to the throne, Justinian I, who changed the laws to be able to marry her.

Once on the throne, Theodora ruled in equality with her husband – some say in place of him. Either way, she played a major role in changes throughout Byzantium. She successfully advocated for the rights of women, creating laws that protected them from being forced into prostitution, eliminating a law that had punished women who committed adultery with death and increasing women's rights in divorce. Theodora's decisive role in political actions can be seen in 532's Nika Revolt, when two political and religious groups united against Justinian. A melee occurred during chariot races at the Hippodrome in Constantinople. Amidst the destruction, Justinian was prepared to flee, but Theodora stepped in and told him to stand his ground. He dispatched forces who brutally quelled the uprising and restored Justinian's authority.

Constantinople's massive Hippodrome stood on the site of modern Istanbul's Sultanahmet Square; almost all that remains of it is the ancient Egyptian obelisk erected within the grounds by Theodosius I in AD 390.

'Trees are not known by their leaves, nor even by their blossoms, but by their fruits.'

Fontevraud Abbey

ELEANOR OF AQUITAINE

Fontevraud-l'Abbaye, France

One of the most powerful rulers in the Middle Ages, Eleanor of Aquitaine (circa 1122–1204) was a rarity, indeed – a woman with absolute dominion over a large swath of Europe. As the duchess of Aquitaine, she controlled what is now mostly southwestern France, and later became the queen of first France and then England, when she married first Louis VII then Henry II. Gorgeous and strong-willed, she was also a patron of the arts.

When Eleanor married her second husband, Henry of Anjou, who became king of England in 1154, she played a large part in the running of his empire as well as her own. She had two daughters with Louis VII and then five sons and three daughters with Henry II. (One of those sons was Richard the Lion Heart.) She led a life of adventure and intrigue – at one point she was imprisoned for 16 years, suspected of betraying her husband Henry's interest in favour of their son. When Henry died, her son Richard named her regent, so she ruled the country while he went to fight the Third Crusade. Eleanor lived out her final years in her territories in Aquitaine, becoming a nun at the abbey at Fontevraud.

◉ Today, visitors can stay at a hotel on the gorgeous abbey grounds.

> **'I prayed every second I was in the barrel except for a few seconds after the fall when I went unconscious.'**

Niagara Falls

ANNIE EDSON TAYLOR

Niagara Falls, USA/Canada

What do you do when you want to retire, but your husband is dead and you are a teacher, so you don't have a lot to retire on? If you're Annie Edson Taylor (1838–1921), you pack yourself into a barrel and let the current take you over Niagara Falls.

Annie had heard of men defying the whirlpool at the bottom of the falls and figured completing a stunt that involved going over the falls themselves could help her raise some funds to retire comfortably. It was to be a PR stunt for the ages. But the Michigan-based schoolteacher wasn't stupid: She did a test run with her cat before going in herself. Niagara the cat reportedly made the trip unscathed, though if Niagara herself had been asked, she may have told a different story.

On 24 October 1901, Annie packed herself into a barrel of her own design, with a mattress for protection, a harness to keep her from jostling around too much and a weighty anvil at the bottom to keep her upright. Ever the hustler, Annie told the newspapers she was 43, though sources confirm she was probably at least 63, and at least one news outlet called her 'aged'. Aged or not, Annie bobbed along the river until her barrel disappeared into the falls. Miraculously, Annie resurfaced and her team quickly pulled the barrel out of the water below. Annie suffered a scratch on her head but was otherwise fine as she was being liberated from her barrel.

Annie was the first person to survive going over the falls. With her stunt, she pioneered women's participation in daredevil activities and, for better or worse, shattered the industry's glass ceiling.

Unfortunately, while the event might have supported the idea that women were just as capable of the same dangerous and ill-advised acts of derring-do as men were, the trip didn't earn Annie the riches she was hoping for. She died destitute and is buried near the falls with her great achievement noted on her tombstone.

📍 Follow the honeymooning couples to Niagara Falls, just half an hour north/northwest of Buffalo, NY on interstate 190.

Neues Schloss

PRINCESS WILHELMINE

Bayreuth, Germany

In the 18th century Bayreuth was a small, German backwater within the Holy Roman Empire. Enter Princess Wilhelmine of Prussia (1709–1758), married off to the margrave's son by her father. Despairing at her new position in the parochial town, the cultivated young princess, the older sister of Frederick the Great, set about transforming it into a centre of the Enlightenment. Handily, her husband came into his inheritance in 1735, and they embarked on a grand building plan, constructing parks and gardens, promoting the arts, founding a university and setting up a salon. Wilhelmine's vision shaped Bayreuth, making it a growing cultural beacon while pushing the court to the verge of bankruptcy in the process. Later, she turned her able mind to politics during the Seven Years' War.

Among her most renowned accomplishments is the Markgräfliches Opernhaus. Lavishly decorated, it opened in 1746 and remains Germany's largest and most spectacular performance space, attracting the attention of Wagner, 114 years after Wilhelmine's death, and convincing him to hold his annual festival in the town. Wilhelmine also set about building herself a new palace, the Neues Schloss, a flamboyant confection, and redecorated the Eremitage, or Old Palace, in rococo style. By the time of her death in 1758, Bayreuth had been completely remodelled, and Wilhelmine hailed as the architect of its regeneration.

📍 Bayreuth is about a 90-minute train ride from Nuremberg.

© Silver Screen Collection / Getty Images

Finca Vigía
AVA GARDNER
Havana, Cuba

Married to actor Mickey Rooney, then to jazz musician Artie Shaw and later to Frank Sinatra, there's no question that Hollywood star Ava Gardner impressed numerous interesting men. But beyond her femme fatale reputation she was no mean actor, almost snaring an Oscar for her role in *The Killers*. She also maintained a long-term friendship with the reclusive Howard Hughes, but it was left to author Ernest Hemingway, another old friend, to provide the best encapsulation of Gardner's appeal. After watching her swimming, minus her swimsuit, in his pool at his wonderful house Finca Vigía on the outskirts of Havana, Cuba, Hemingway ordered his staff: 'The water is not to be emptied.'

➡ To reach San Francisco de Paula, take metro bus P-7 (Alberro) from Parque de la Fraternidad in Centro Habana.

Nadezhda Durova Statue
NADEZHDA DUROVA
Yelabuga, Russia

In the town of Yelabuga in Tatarstan, an equestrian statue stands proud in the city centre, revealed to be that of a woman in military uniform on closer inspection. This upright figure is none other than the celebrated Nadezhda Durova (1783–1866).

The daughter of a Russian major, Durova was brought up around soldiers, riding horses and playing with guns. At the age of 24, the fierce patriot disguised herself as a man and fought in the Prussian campaign under the alias Alexander Sokolov and later in the Napoleonic wars. Tsar Alexander I took a personal interest in her exploits and awarded her the pseudonym Alexandrov.

➡ Find the statue at the intersection of Ulitsa Durova and Ulitsa Kazanskaya.

Hasenheide Park

TRÜMMERFRAUEN

Berlin, Germany

In Berlin's Hasenheide Park, there's a statue of a woman sitting on a pile of bricks. She's holding a hammer and looking upwards exhaustedly. The monument is dedicated to the *Trümmerfrauen* (rubble women) who completed the cleanup and reconstruction of German cities in WWII's aftermath. It's a well-known sight to summer joggers and picnickers, but what you might not realise at first is that it's because of women like this that Berlin exists as we know it today.

Across the country, bombings and firestorms had wiped out or damaged about half of all infrastructure. With many German men dead or prisoners of war, the Allies ordered all women between ages 15 and 50 to tear down the ruins and collect bricks for rebuilding. It was hard manual labour using sledgehammers and picks. In Berlin alone, around 60,000 women toiled in the soot and ash for typically nine hours a day, earning minimal pay and food ration cards.

Sculpted by Katharina Szelinski-Singer, the shell limestone sculpture in Hasenheide Park was commissioned in 1952 when 32 'rubble women' received the Federal Cross of Merit. In 1955 it was first erected on the Rixdorfer Hoehe, a mountainous tribute to the Trümmerfrauen who constructed postwar Germany out of debris, stones and steel by their hard work. In 1986, it was moved to its current spot for better visibility by all the passersby in the busy park.

📍 The monument is located near the park's northern Graefestrasse entrance, closest to Hermannplatz station.

© aluxum / Getty Images

Kyoto Imperial Palace

TOMOE GOZEN

Kyoto, Japan

In Japan's legendary samurai tradition, rare but celebrated are the *onna-bugeisha* or female warriors. Tomoe Gozen (1157–1247) is the most storied of these due to her role at the centre of the Genpei Wars fought by her husband and chronicled in the *Heike Monogatari*. She even led 300 samurai at the head of her own force.

Jidai Matsuri, one of Kyoto's big three annual festivals, is held here each fall and features more than 2000 people dressed in costumes ranging from the 8th to the 19th centuries parading from the Kyoto Imperial Palace to Heian-jingū. Attendees will surely spy women dressed as Tomoe Gozen among the throng.

📍 The Jidai Matsuri, or Festival of Ages, is held each October.

Trinity Cemetery

LILI ELBE

Dresden, Germany

Lili Elbe, born Einar Magnus Andreas Wegener in Denmark in 1882, was an artist who is also one of the earliest documented recipients of gender confirmation surgery. She frequently modelled for her wife Gerda Wegener, also a painter and a staunch supporter of Lili's evolution. Lili's autobiography, *Lili: A Portrait of the First Sex Change*, provided the material for a novel and film based on her story, *The Danish Girl*. Eventually Lili travelled to Germany in 1930 to have a series of gender reassignment surgeries. At the time these medical procedures were in their infancy, and the fourth operation Lili underwent (to implant a womb) sadly proved to be fatal; she died in Dresden in 1931. Lili Elbe's grave in Dresden's Trinity Cemetery was renovated in 2016, after the release of the critically acclaimed 2015 movie about her life.

If visiting Lili and Gerda's home country of Denmark, the Vejle Art Museum holds some of their artworks.

4

Sites for
GODDESS
WORSHIP

1 PACHAMAMA

Pachamama Temple, Isla Amantani, Peru

On the Peruvian island of Amantaní on Lake Titicaca, twin mountain peaks Pachamama and Pachatata rise up from the ground, their terraced hillsides lined with fields of quinoa, potatoes and wheat. The island's residents, descendants of the ancient Aymara culture, make sacrifices to Pachamama to protect their crops, hiking to the peak of Pachamama to the temple that overlooks the island. Throughout the Andean communities of South America, there's no female figure more important than Pachamama – also known as 'Mother Earth'. In ancient Inca mythology, Pachamama is the goddess of time and fertility: she controls the sun, the moon, and the movement of water, managing the harvest and thereby making life on earth possible.

2 ATHENA

Parthenon, Athens, Greece

Designed to be the pre-eminent monument of the Acropolis, the Parthenon epitomises ancient Greece's glory. Meaning 'virgin's apartment', it's dedicated to Athena Parthenos, the goddess embodying the power and prestige of the city. The largest Doric temple ever completed in Greece, the Parthenon took 15 years to build. Completed by 438 BC, it was built on the highest ground of the Acropolis. The Parthenon had a dual purpose: to house the great statue of Athena commissioned by Pericles and to serve as the new treasury. It was built on the site of at least three earlier temples dedicated to Athena. Goddess of wisdom and warfare, patron of Athens, she continues to represent intelligence thanks to her birth story, springing from the forehead of Zeus.

MEENAKSHI

Meenakshi Amman Temple, Madurai, India

The colourful abode of the triple-breasted warrior goddess Meenakshi in Tamil Nadu is generally considered the peak of South Indian temple architecture. Meenakshi Temple is a 17th-century temple on a 6-hectare (15-acre) complex featuring 12 tall *gopurams* (towers), encrusted with a staggering array of gods, goddesses, demons and heroes (1511 on the massive south gopuram alone). According to legend, the beautiful Meenakshi (a version of Parvati) was born with three breasts and this prophecy: her superfluous breast would melt away when she met her husband. This happened when she met Shiva and took her place as his consort. Every evening, an incense-clouded procession carries an icon of Sundareswarar (Shiva) to Meenakshi's shrine to spend the night.

ARTEMIS

Temple of Artemis, Selçuk, Turkey

In an empty field to the west of present-day Selçuk's centre, one lone reconstructed pillar is all that remains of the massive Artemision (or Temple of Artemis), one of the Seven Wonders of the Ancient World in then-Greek Ephesus. At its zenith, the temple counted 127 columns; today, the only way to get any sense of its grandeur is to visit the Library of Celcus at Ephesus or Didyma's better-preserved Temple of Apollo (at a 'mere' 122 columns). The temple was damaged by flooding and various invaders during its 1000-year lifespan. It was always rebuilt, a sign of the great love Ephesians felt for their fertility goddess (Diana to the Romans). Her cult brought immense wealth to the city from pilgrims and benefactors who included the greatest rulers of the era.

'Adventure is worthwhile in itself.'

Amelia Earhart Monument

AMELIA EARHART

Burry Port, Wales

Amelia Earhart's memorial in Burry Port marks the nearby landing of the first woman to cross the Atlantic by plane on 17 June 1928, though visitors may note that Burry Port and neighbouring Pwll have been at loggerheads for years over which settlement deserves the accolade of being the site of the famed aviator's landing point.

It is actually a complex issue. When the history-making aircraft alighted after the flight from Newfoundland on the sandy South Wales coast, Earhart and crew were informed they were in 'Pwll Inlet'. Consequently, Pwll has a Blue Plaque remembering the event. But the plane touched down on water and was towed to Burry Port where the crew first set foot on land. So Burry Port, incensed at the Pwll plaque, decided to commemorate Earhart in a bigger, better way with a full-fledged monument. Be careful, all ye Earhart fans who enter here, which camp you voice support for. Arrival at Burry Port (or Pwll) made Earhart the first female to have crossed the Atlantic by air, a feat she would one-up in making the first solo transatlantic air crossing by a woman in 1932. Then, she touched down in a field in Derry, Northern Ireland. Howland Island's Earhardt Light is also named after the aviator, who disappeared somewhere near the Pacific Ocean isle.

📍 It is about 200m (0.1 miles) from Pembrey & Burry Port station to the monument.

São Miguel Fortress

QUEEN NZINGA

Luanda, Angola

Queen Nzinga (circa 1583–1663) towers over Angolan history. She was born with her umbilical cord around her neck, and her survival against the odds as an infant would herald a future where she overcame all challenges. The Portuguese had already established a base in neighbouring Luanda when she was born in the kingdom of Ndongo, home to the Mbundu people. She took control of her father's throne against opposition to a woman ruler after regrouping in the territory of Matamba and forging an accord with the Imbangala. She fought Portuguese influence by cutting off slave trade routes and even taking in refugees from slavers, eventually forming an alliance with the Dutch to hold her ground.

Today, her statue stands in front of São Miguel fortress, built by the Portuguese in 1576. It's an appropriate place for it: São Miguel fortress also contains the Museum of the Armed Forces, which displays military equipment from the Angolan War of Independence. Queen Nzinga's pride of place outside compares to the statues of former Portuguese rulers to be found inside of the fort, where they were removed from their original locations in Luanda once Portuguese control ended. A major port for the slave trade to Brazil, São Miguel represents the height of Portuguese influence that Queen Nzinga fought against with such dedication, as well as the eventual return of the land to its people.

📍 Luanda's oldest surviving building, the fort (its modern entrance gate pictured below) offers sweeping views of the city below.

Diana Memorial Fountain, Hyde Park

DIANA, PRINCESS OF WALES

London, England

'Carry out a random act of kindness, with no expectation of reward, safe in the knowledge that one day someone might do the same for you.'

Few people resonated as strongly with the British public as the late Diana, Princess of Wales. Shock and mourning at her tragic death led to a blanket of flowers outside Kensington Palace, and in 2004, a memorial fountain was established in her memory within nearby Hyde Park. The memorial fountain was envisaged by the designer Kathryn Gustafson as a 'moat without a castle', draped 'like a necklace' around the southwestern edge of Hyde Park near the Serpentine Bridge. The circular double stream is composed of 545 pieces of Cornish granite, its waters drawn from a chalk aquifer more than 100m (328ft) below ground. Those who remember her charitable work and bewitching smile can also visit Hyde Park's Diana Memorial Playground, the Diana Memorial Walk at St James's Palace and the White Garden within the Kensington Palace grounds.

⬤ Hyde Park and Kensington Gardens cover a total area of 253 hectares (625 acres).

'Nefertiti is like Athena born from the brow of Zeus, a head-heavy armored goddess.'
—Camille Paglia

Temple of Amun, Karnak
NEFERTITI
Thebes, Egypt

Nefertiti (circa 1370–1330 BC) was one of the most powerful women in the world during the 14th century BC. She was the mysterious queen of Egypt, married to King Akhenaten. During her time in power, she played an important role in the cult of the sun god. She even took over otherwise kingly duties to serve as a priest in the worship of the god, who was called Aton or Aten. Together, she and the king elevated the cult to extraordinary status, making Aton the premier god in the Egyptian pantheon. Her name translates as 'A Beautiful Woman Has Come', and Nefertiti is depicted in many stunning works of art from the period. She's easy to recognise with her special crown, a blue, high, flat-topped headdress. Many of the artworks show her as an affectionate partner to the king, and some show her wreaking vengeance on her foes.

Nefertiti was also apparently perceived as a living fertility goddess herself. There are some historians who believed she ruled along with her husband rather than being strictly his consort, or that she may have ruled after his death. Nefertiti gave birth to six daughters, three of them in Thebes – and two of them became queens of Egypt in their own right. At the apex of her powers, in the twelfth year of the reign of Akhenaten, all records of Nefertiti disappear. No one knows for sure what became of her, but her legacy lives on in the art that represents her to the modern world.

During their reign Nefertiti and King Akhenaten ruled in Thebes, where the Donation Stelae in the Temple of Amun bestows the title 'Wife of the Gods' on Nefertiti.

© TTstudio / Shutterstock

Borgia Apartments
LUCREZIA BORGIA
V̌atican City, Italy

The daughter of future pope Alexander VI and his mistress, Lucrezia Borgia (1480–1519) was born into an Italian family of vast wealth and influence. Alive during the Italian Renaissance, Borgia lived a life surrounded by political machinations. She was well educated, speaking Italian, French, Greek and Latin, but her value to her clan also rested on her ability to form advantageous marriages. Lucrezia's famous beauty was a great aid in this; she even served as a model for Il Pinturicchio's fresco *St Catherine's Disputation* in her father's Vatican apartments. When the husbands were no longer useful to her family, the infamous Borgias would manage a way to be rid of them – it is widely believed that they had her second husband killed. After the death of her father and a more stable third marriage with Alfonso d'Este, Duke of Ferrara, Lucrezia Borgia's own life normalised and she became a patron of the arts. As time has passed, it has become increasingly unclear whether she was an equal actor in the schemes of her father and her brother, Cesare. Perhaps she was a pawn in their political games. But countless salacious stories, from a play by Victor Hugo to an opera by Donizetti, depict her as a seductress who would poison those who stood in her way.

📍 Trace the path of Lucrezia Borgia and her family in Rome in places such as Palazzo Orsini and of course the Vatican (pictured above).

Emancipation Park

NANNY OF THE MAROONS

New Kingston, Jamaica

While not much has been written about her in the history books, her legacy largely carried by oral accounts, Queen Nanny of the Maroons is considered one of Jamaica's most important military heroes. Born in Ghana and sold into slavery, Nanny was sent to Jamaica to work on its plantations. She was able to escape to the Blue Mountains, where she founded the Maroon community of Nanny Town. From there, she led the community in active resistance against the British colonists and is said to have freed hundreds of enslaved people during her lifetime. Her leadership was of pivotal importance in the First Maroon War (1720–1739), during which she was killed in battle in 1733. Today, her likeness appears on the Jamaican $500 note, and she is also Jamaica's only officially designated female National Hero. You can also visit monuments to Queen Nanny in Moore Town, as well as in Kingston's Emancipation Park.

📍 Head to the Moore Town Maroon Cultural Center to learn about Moore Town's history before hiking to nearby Nanny Falls, a brilliant cascade of water named for the town's heroine.

Bouboulina Museum

LASKARINA BOUBOULINA

Spetses, Greece

The Greek freedom fighter and heroine Laskarina Bouboulina, often called simply Bouboulina, was born around 1771. The daughter of a sea captain, she would become known for her daring exploits as commander of an armada fighting the Ottoman occupation. Because the tall tales of Bouboulina's adventures are featured in many florid ballads and plays, it's difficult to weed out truth from fantasy. But it is known that growing up she absorbed maritime skills, likely from her father. When her first husband died, she took over his four ships and led them, as their commander, in the Greek War of Independence. She was a daring, swashbuckling leader, who racked up victories, and would often leave her ship to fight on land as well. But she was also an accomplished negotiator who would bargain for settlements to preserve lives.

Larger-than-life Bouboulina was the mother of six children and she was widowed by both of her husbands. She herself died in 1825, in the midst of a family vendetta, killed by a bullet in her home – possibly stray or possibly intentional. You can visit that home today, a charming museum on the island of Spetses. Visits are by guided tour, with the hours posted on boards at the museum and around Spetses' Dapia harbour.

📍 In addition to the museum (pictured opposite), there's a statue of Bouboulina on the harbour, opposite the Hotel Poseidonion.

Zöe Mosaic

ZÖE PORPHYROGENITA

Hagia Sophia, Turkey

Take a close look at the gold and glass Zöe Mosaic at Istanbul's magnificent Hagia Sophia, the centre of Byzantine life in then-Constantinople, and you'll get an insight into the colourful life of Empress Zöe. The mosaic depicts the iconic ruler to the right of Jesus, with her husband Constantine IX to his left. But there are traces that all three heads have been tampered with. This is potentially because Constantine IX was Zöe's third husband and updates may have been made when her previous spouses perished.

Zöe Porphyrogenita was born in AD 978 to Emperor Constantine VIII and betrothed at age 23 to Holy Roman Emperor Otto III. Alas, Otto died before Zöe's ship reached Rome and she was sent back to live in the Great Palace of Constantinople until her father died and she was declared the Byzantine Empress at age 50. When her first husband died mysteriously in the bath after their marriage, Zöe married her teenaged lover Michael on the same day. After he also died, her adopted heir banished Zöe to a monastery as he took the throne. But he was unpopular with the subjects and after a revolt, Zöe re-took the throne to co-rule with her younger sister Theodora. When she married her third husband, Constantine, the three ruled in an unprecedented tripartite arrangement until her death at age 72 in 1050.

◉ Find the mosaic on the upper level of Hagia Sophia on the wall furthest from the main entrance.

Rose Bowl

BRANDI CHASTAIN

Pasadena, USA

Twenty years later, it remains perhaps the most iconic photograph of a female athlete ever: US defender Brandi Chastain dropped to her knees, her pumped fist clutching the jersey she'd just ripped off, baring a now-famous black sports bra and muscles underneath. Chastain had just hammered home the winning penalty kick in the Americans' nail-biting 5–4 victory against China in the 1999 Women's World Cup. But the moment illustrated something so much bigger than just a championship: it showed a woman revelling in her athletic victory against all stereotypes. In 2004 FIFA, soccer's governing body, banned players from removing their jerseys on the field, making it even harder to imagine Chastain's bra-baring moment of glory ever being topped.

📍 Located northeast of downtown Los Angeles in Pasadena, the Rose Bowl underwent a $183 million renovation that was completed in 2016.

House of Commons

JO COX

London, England

Visitors to the House of Commons in London may spot a plaque in the shape of a small shield dedicated to Jo Cox. It was designed by her two small children and features two white and two red roses, representing the four members of the Cox family and Ms Cox's alliance to the Labour Party and to Yorkshire. Members of Parliament killed while in office are commemorated using such shields; Ms Cox was murdered in 2016 by a far-right extremist while on her way to work. The plaque bears the motto 'more in common' from Ms Cox's maiden speech in the Commons.

📍 The plaque is displayed in the Commons chamber in the Palace of Westminster, the seat of British government.

ZENOBIA

Palmyra, Syria

The ancient city of Palmyra was known as the Pearl of the Desert. An oasis that had long served as a waypoint for Silk Road caravans, by the 3rd century it was a centre of culture and sophistication whose markets were overflowing with luxury goods like jade, spices and silk. A place fit for an empress, really. And that was exactly what Palmyra's queen, Zenobia, planned to make of herself.

Zenobia had come to the throne after the assassination of her husband, the king. He had been an accomplished military leader, and the queen had often accompanied him to the front lines to learn the art of making war. As comfortable in intellectual spheres as she was on the battlefield, Zenobia had a keen interest in philosophy and spoke four languages.

By the time Zenobia became queen, the Romans had been occupying Palmyra for over two centuries. The empire, though, was churning with internal problems. When a succession crisis deepened the chaos in Rome, the queen saw her people's chance at freedom. Donning an elaborate diadem and her late husband's military cloak, she took it.

Zenobia spent three years securing Palmyra's borders and building up its military. Then she began invading other parts of the Roman Empire, conquering Arabia and then Egypt. Soon, the Palmyrene Empire covered most of the eastern Mediterranean.

The Romans retaliated, of course. Two years after declaring herself queen of Egypt, Zenobia was forced to retreat. Eventually the Emperor Aurelian's forces captured her and paraded her through the streets, humiliated and bound in golden chains. But for one brief moment she had held her own against the mighty Roman Empire. She was a fierce, ambitious, and brilliant woman, more than deserving of the title empress.

BY ANNE THÉRIAULT

Queens of Infamy

Syria's civil war led to the destruction and looting of many sites, but Unesco is leading current renovation efforts in Palmyra with an eye to tourists returning to the site in the near future.

© luxxio / Shutterstock

Oristano

ELEONORA D'ARBOREA

Sardinia, Italy

In the heart of the historic centre of Oristano, Sardinia, stands a commanding woman, proud and tall, hand pointed to the sky. This elegant statue from 1881 commemorates one of Italy's most powerful and respected leaders — Eleonora d'Arborea (1347–1404). Originally born in Catalunya, Spain, d'Arborea was appointed a judge here in 1383 and she held sway on the island of Sardinia until her death.

She was one of the most powerful of the Sardinian judges and is perhaps most known for her creation of the Carta de Logu or Charter of Law in 1392. With that, she completely overhauled the judicial system and local norms. One extremely powerful piece of that legislation gave daughters and sons the same inheritance rights. Revolutionary! She also fought the Aragonese who were aiming to control the region, uniting Sardinia in the battle, but ultimately losing the fight.

Eleanora d'Arborea also made it illegal to poach birds (the first ruler in history to do so) and hence the local Eleonora's falcon, *Falco eleonorae*, was later named after her. You can still find them nesting on the island in spring and summer.

On Isola di San Pietro, just off the southwest coast of Sardinia, gaze wide-eyed at Eleonora's falcons at Cala Fico.

Saint Brigid's Cathedral

SAINT BRIGID

Kildare, Ireland

In Irish history, churches have not always been women-friendly places, but St Brigid's Cathedral in Kildare has always been different. When Brigid (451–525) founded her monastery here around 480, it became a hub of activity where women of all backgrounds could live and work, offering a rare alternative to life as a wife and mother. After a steep climb to the top of the round tower on its grounds, visitors will find that the town of Kildare is still surrounded by the same unspoiled, green rolling hills Brigid would have travelled through. She wouldn't recognise the restored medieval structure that stands here today (although her story is depicted in its stained-glass windows) but the remains of 'Brigid's Kitchen', a stone vault just behind the gates, would be familiar. The sign marks it as a burial vault, but it was also once the site of a sacred pagan fire kept burning by women in honour of a Celtic goddess long before Brigid came. She Christianised the ritual and her order continued to keep the fire going until the Reformation. This place has belonged to women since before recorded history and their traces will not be forgotten easily.

📍 Moore Abbey Woods is a short drive away and is a hidden gem of serene, untouched woodland.

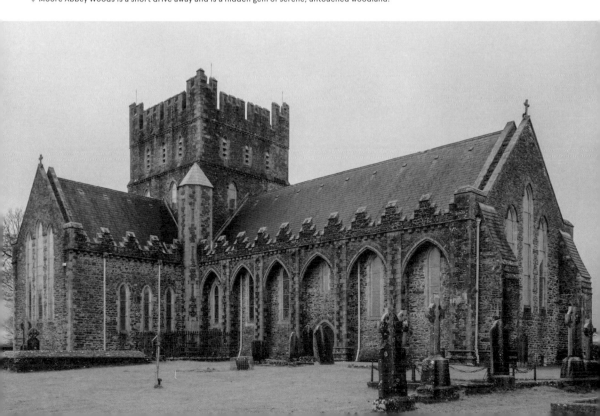

Rozafa Fortress

QUEEN TEUTA

Shkodër, Albania

With spectacular views over the city and Lake Shkodra, the Rozafa Fortress is the most impressive sight in Shkodër. Founded by the Illyrians in antiquity and rebuilt much later by the Venetians and then the Turks, this was one of the Illyrian Queen Teuta's main bases in the region, from which she waged her war against the Romans. Often regarded as a pirate, Queen Teuta led the Illyrian Ardiaei tribe in a spirited defense of their land in present-day Albania and Montenegro. Her reign, from approximately 231 to 227 BC, saw a period of Illyrian raids on Roman merchant vessels from the Adriatic to the Ionian seas, capturing ports as they went.

While Illyrian resistance to the Roman fleet didn't last long, Teuta's legend survived the centuries; she's said to have committed suicide on the Bay of Kotor rather than give in to Roman rule after a forced retreat north from the fortress in Shkodër. Risan, her last stronghold, barely shows any mark of her presence today. Nor is there much left to see inside Rozafa castle itself, save the ruins of various structures and the impressive walls, all created by later rulers of this land. Nevertheless the proud history of its long-ago queen in antiquity still echoes. The castle itself now takes its name from a legend of another woman, Rozafa, supposedly walled into the foundations.

📍 Risan on the Bay of Kotor in Montenegro was the site of Queen Teuta's other main fortress, but few Illyrian remains have been discovered there as yet.

© Keystone Features / Getty Images

Motherhouse

MOTHER TERESA

Kolkata, India

For many people, Mother Teresa (1910–1997) was the living image of human compassion and sacrifice. Born Agnes Gonxha Bojaxhiu to Albanian parents in then-Ottoman Üsküp (now Skopje in Macedonia), she joined the Irish Order of Loreto nuns and worked for more than a decade teaching in Kolkata. Horrified by the city's spiralling poverty, she established a new order, the Missionaries of Charity, and founded refuges for the destitute and dying. The first of these opened in 1952. Although the order swiftly expanded into an international charity, Mother Teresa herself continued to live in absolute simplicity. She was awarded the Nobel Peace Prize in 1979, beatified by the Vatican in 2003 and eventually made a saint in 2016.

However, there are some who detract and question the social worker's call of duty. Feminist author Germaine Greer has accused Mother Teresa of religious imperialism, while journalist Christopher Hitchens' book, *The Missionary Position*, decried donations from dictators and corrupt tycoons. Many have also questioned the order's minimal medical background as well as Teresa's staunch views against contraception. And as recently as 2018, a Missionaries of Charity home in the neighbouring state of Jharkhand was embroiled in a scandal involving selling babies for adoption. Regardless, her defenders continue to look up to Mother Teresa for her lifelong mission to offer care and dignity to the dying and the destitute, inspiring others to follow in her path. A regular flow of pilgrims visits the Missionaries of Charity's 'Motherhouse' to pay homage at Mother (and now Saint) Teresa's large, sober tomb.

From Sudder St, walk for about 15 minutes along Alimuddin St, then two minutes south. It's in the second alley to the right.

Westminster Abbey

QUEEN ELIZABETH I

London, England

Third in line after the death of Henry VIII, Elizabeth I came to the throne unexpectedly. Her reign inherited a nasty mess of religious strife and divided loyalties, but after an uncertain start she gained confidence and turned the country around. Refusing marriage, she borrowed biblical motifs and became known as the Virgin Queen, perhaps the first English monarch to create a cult image.

The big moments in her 45-year reign included the naval defeat of the Spanish Armada, the far-flung explorations of English seafarers Walter Raleigh and Francis Drake, and the expansion of England's trading network, including newly established colonies on the east coast of America. There was also a cultural flourishing, thanks to writers such as William Shakespeare and Christopher Marlowe. (She also held Mary Queen of Scots under arrest for nearly 19 years before ordering her execution in 1587.) The Elizabethan era of 1558–1603 stands out as a golden age of peace and prosperity for the realm its queen oversaw. Today, she is buried in Westminster Abbey's Lady Chapel alongside the tomb of her half sister, Mary I.

⬤ Westminster Abbey is what is called a 'royal peculiar', administered by the Crown and the coronation church since 1066; it holds daily services as well as having visiting hours for tourists Mon-Sat.

© John Stillwel / Getty Images

'I didn't want fame or fortune. But I did want my own identity.'
-Naomi Parker Fraley

WWII Home Front National Historical Park

ROSIE THE RIVETER

Richmond, USA

Rosie the Riveter is one of the most beloved American cultural Icons of the 20th century, having helped galvanise some 12 million US women who entered the workforce during WWII to replace enlisted men. Since her wartime debut, Rosie's powerful image has only gained resonance, constantly being remixed and repurposed. But as recognised as Rosie is, the actual woman behind the fist-pumping, bandanna-clad legend has been the subject of considerable debate, partly because the character has been linked to the 1943 hit song 'Rosie the Riveter', a Norman Rockwell painting, and a wartime industrial poster based off a photograph. In 2016 a six-year research project by scholar James J Jenkins definitively named Naomi Parker Fraley, who had worked at the machine shop at the Naval Air Station in Alameda, California, as the original 'Rosie'.

Fraley passed away in 2018, but her memory – and that of an entire generation of hardworking women – lives on at the Rosie the Riveter/WWII Home Front National Historical Park in Richmond, California. Every year, the park's annual Rosie Rally Homefront Festival draws hundreds of visitors, many of them women wearing denim work shirts and red polka-dotted bandannas, to celebrate the achievements of America's home-front women workers and their 'can-do' spirit.

Just north of Oakland, the Rosie the Riveter/WWII Home Front National Historical Park in Richmond, where 56 wartime industries were once represented, offers a fascinating look at the efforts of home-front workers during the war.

Knife River Villages

SACAGAWEA

Stanton, USA

Sacagawea was still a little girl, just 11 or 12, when she was kidnapped by raiders from a neighbouring tribe. She was barely older when a French-Canadian fur trader took her as a child bride. She was dead of typhus before her 25th birthday. Yet because of her strength and intelligence, Sacagawea's story soars above these miserable circumstances. Born to the Shoshone people in Idaho, Sacagawea was living with her captor-husband in the Knife River Villages of North Dakota when Meriwether Lewis and William Clark arrived. On an expedition to map the American West, they hired Sacagawea's husband as an interpreter. Sacagawea came too, her infant son on her back, and helped the party communicate with the Shoshone as the party headed for the Pacific Coast. Her bravery and resourcefulness were legendary – jumping into a river to rescue items from a capsized boat, saving the party from starvation by cooking native plants.

Today, the Knife River Villages where she lived are a National Historic Site, with a museum and reconstructed homes and gardens. See objects made by the Plains Indians, and walk the Village Trail through the wooded bottomlands to the ruins of Awatixa Village, where Sacagawea first encountered Lewis and Clark. Some native oral traditions say that, rather than dying young, Sacagawea returned to the Shoshone, dying an honoured matriarch at 95. We devoutly hope so.

The Knife River Villages are in Stanton, North Dakota, north of Bismarck.

Kilmuir Cemetery

FLORA MACDONALD

Isle of Skye, Scotland

On a low green hill on Skye's lonely Trotternish Peninsula stands one of Scotland's most striking cemeteries. It is of note for one particular reason: the grave of Flora MacDonald. On her resting place, marked by a lofty Celtic cross, a plaque sums up this lassie's history-changing act: 'Preserver of Prince Charles Edward Stuart'. Mr Stuart, of course, is better known as Bonnie Prince Charlie, or the Young Pretender, Scotland's last attempt to return a Scottish king to their throne.

MacDonald's heroics entailed ferrying the prince, disguised as her maid, over to Skye: this enabled him to evade capture after the Battle of Culloden and return to safety in France. But she put herself and her family at grave risk from the English troops hunting down the prince. Indeed, a fortnight afterwards, she was arrested and imprisoned in the Tower of London. But the way in which she had saved Bonnie Prince Charlie's life captured public imagination, and she had many sympathisers, including then-heir to the throne Frederick, Prince of Wales. Released in 1747, she lived until 1790.

Much about MacDonald helping the prince escape has passed into the realm of legend. And she did not reignite the Stuart cause. But the risky ride she gave the Young Pretender meant Jacobite hopes did not completely die for a while longer.

📍 Kilmuir Cemetery is 373km (232 miles) northwest of Glasgow and 35km (21.5 miles) northwest of Portree.

Linlithgow Palace

MARY, QUEEN OF SCOTS

Linlithgow, Scotland

The last crowned monarch of Scotland before the union of the English and Scottish crowns, Mary, Queen of Scots (1542–1587) was one of the most contentious and colourful figures in the history of British royals. Married as a teenager to the man who would become king of France, as well as to two key players in the battle of intrigues raging within politics in 16th-century Britain, she was at various points queen consort of France and a severe threat to the throne of Queen Elizabeth I, who would eventually order her execution. But most of all she was a forthright individual who endured everything thrown at her and, a number of times, bounced back under hard circumstances: from being widowed at 18 to leading troops to battle to being abducted and imprisoned.

Mary's birthplace, the bulky ruin of Linlithgow Palace beside a loch in lovely West Lothian parkland, is one of several locations to have poignant associations with the monarch; she was only six days old when her father King James V of Scotland died. Many of the parts you see today the young Mary too would have seen: the north quarter, where she was likely born, and the courtyard fountain, added only four years before her birth. It is a moving spot to absorb what day-to-day life might have been like for Mary and other Scottish royals in a mightily turbulent era.

📍 Linlithgow train station, on the Edinburgh-Glasgow line, is walking distance southeast of the palace.

© TreasureGalore / Shutterstock

Memorial Statue
CORAZON AQUINO

Manila, Philippines

The widow of the assassinated opposition figure and senator Beningo 'Nino' Aquino, Corazon 'Cory' Aquino took over her husband's mantle on his death and led the People Power revolution to overthrow the dictator Ferdinand Marcos. She became the first woman elected president of the Philippines in 1986. As president, one of Aquino's first acts was to oversee adoption of the 1987 constitution, which returned civil liberties to a country freed from its long period of military rule. After a tenure in office that steered past coup attempts and natural disasters, Aquino peacefully turned over power to her successor, having re-established democratic norms. She continued her advocacy once out of office through involvement in multiple charities. Upon her death of cancer in 2009, Aquino was given a state funeral and mourned by hundreds of thousands of Filipinos.

📍 The bronze statue of Corazon Aquino sits outside Manila Hotel on Roxas Boulevard, across from a statue of her assassinated husband.

Jhansi Fort

RANI LAKSHMIBAI

Uttar Pradesh, India

If ever there was a woman steeped in myth, it would be Rani Lakshmibai, the widow queen of Jhansi, who strode into battle against the British in 1857. The most dramatic retellings of her story would have her plunging from the Jhansi Fort walls, with her adopted son strapped on her back, thick into the heart of battle; preferring death to dishonour. The truth is probably more prosaic, but the warrior queen did die in battle against a vast British army who had indiscriminately slaughtered 3000 of her people.

By all accounts, Jhansi's queen was a startling woman, well ahead of her era. She learned to read and write, skills that were considered useless to high-caste Brahmin women of her time. She also learned archery, shooting, *mallakhamb* (an Indian form of gymnastics), horsemanship, and was a dab hand with a sword. When she became queen, she rebuffed attacks against her kingdom from surrounding kings who thought she was easy prey, what with her being a woman and all. And we know that she did all these things, most likely in her teens or in her early 20s. General Hugh Rose, against whom she flew into battle, is said to have written rather grudgingly that she was 'the best and bravest of the rebels'. Today, there is a museum inside her beloved Jhansi Fort dedicated to the Queen, which displays the weapons of this fierce woman in pride of place.

 If you brave public transport, the Jhansi Museum bus stop will point you right to the Jhansi Fort.

Children's Peace Monument
SADAKO SASAKI
Ḥiroshima, Japan

The Children's Peace Monument was inspired by Sadako Sasaki, who was just two years old at the time of the atomic bomb. At age 11 she developed leukaemia, and decided to fold 1000 paper cranes. In Japan, the crane is a symbol of longevity and happiness, and she believed if she folded 1000 she would recover. Sadly she died before reaching her goal, but her classmates folded the rest. A monument was built in 1958 to remind visitors from across the world of the dangers of nuclear weapons. Sadako's story inspired a nationwide spate of paper-crane folding that continues to this day. Surrounding the monument are strings of thousands of colourful paper cranes, sent here by schoolchildren from around the country and all over the world.

📍 The Flame of Peace, a feature of the pond in Peace Memorial Park, will be extinguished only once every nuclear weapon on earth has been destroyed.

Shibden Hall

ANNE LISTER

Yorkshire, England

The bold and brazen landowner Anne Lister, who became financially independent after inheriting Shibden Hall from her uncle in 1832, was a prolific diarist. The writing she left behind totalled more than four million words, but the portion of the diaries detailing her (many) lesbian affairs with other women was written in code for her own protection. Its explosive content was kept hidden for over a hundred years, until a local historian called Helena Whitbread stumbled across it in the 1980s. Lister's Yorkshire home Shibden Hall is now open to visitors, many drawn by the *Gentleman Jack* TV series based on Lister's life. Lister had numerous love affairs, including a long-running relationship with a Yorkshire neighbour, Ann Walker. The two would exchange rings in York's Holy Trinity Church in 1834. Able to resist bowing to convention due to her independent status, gender-bending Lister unrepentantly and with verve lived as she saw fit.

Accessible by local bus, the manor is surrounded by parklands with walking trails, a miniature railway and a boating lake. Hours are currently seasonal, but may become year-round in the future.

10

Queer PIONEERS

Women who rock the world don't always get the credit they deserve, especially when they're LGBT+. These 10 women and gender nonconforming people made an indelible mark on the places they lived, and their stories still resonate.

1 ALICE DUNBAR-NELSON

An African American poet associated with the Harlem Renaissance as well as a journalist and activist, Dunbar-Nelson had three husbands in her life, but also numerous women lovers. Her activism included organising for women's suffrage and campaigning for the Dyer Anti-Lynching bill.

2 ELISA SÁNCHEZ LORIGA & MARCELA GRACIA IBEAS

A century before same-sex marriage was legalised in Spain, the windswept port town of A Coruña was the setting of a lesbian wedding in 1901 – Elisa's sharp tuxedo and a forged birth certificate were enough to fool the priest.

3 EDITH WINDSOR

When the US Supreme Court ruled in Edith's favour in 2013's United States v Windsor case, it was a huge leap forward in same-sex marriage, recognising the validity of Edith Windsor's marriage under US federal law and striking down the Defense of Marriage Act.

4 GLADYS BENTLEY

Walk through Harlem in NYC and you're in the old stomping ground of cross-dressing blues superstar Gladys Bentley (1907–1960). Her voice and stage presence won her fans, while her 1931 interracial lesbian marriage made waves.

5 GEORGINA BEYER

Elected the world's first openly trans mayor in 1995 and later the world's first openly trans parliamentary member in 2000, Georgina's past experience as a marginalised sex worker led her to give crucial support to New Zealand's groundbreaking Prostitution Reform Act 2003.

RADCLYFFE HALL

The medieval East Sussex town of Rye bears the footprints of English writer Radclyffe Hall (1880–1943), whose literary masterpiece *The Well of Loneliness* was subject to an obscenity trial for its lesbian themes.

BARBARA GITTINGS

Founder of the NYC chapter of the Daughters of Bilitis, the USA's first lesbian rights organisation, Barbara Gittings (1932–2007) was a tireless activist who exposed government discrimination against LGBT employees.

CHRISTINE JORGENSEN

Despite encountering vicious discrimination after undergoing gender confirmation surgery and hormone treatment in 1951 Copenhagen, American Christine Jorgensen (1926–1989) used her platform to advocate for trans rights.

ALBERTA HUNTER

The raunchy lyrics of velvety-voiced Alberta Hunter (1895–1984) may mention her 'handy man', but the Tennessee jazz singer-songwriter was privately a lesbian. Inducted into Memphis' Music Hall of Fame, her songs still rock the bars on entertainment strip Beale St.

MARSHA P JOHNSON

Every rainbow-clad attendee of an American Pride march owes a debt to Marsha P Johnson (1945–1992), a gender nonconforming activist who was on the battle lines of the Stonewall riot of 1969.

'Equality means more than passing laws. The struggle is really won in the hearts and minds of the community, where it really counts.'–*Barbara Gittings*

In Her Footsteps
February 2020
Published by Lonely Planet Global Limited
CRN 554153
www.lonelyplanet.com
10 9 8 7 6 5 4 3 2 1
Printed in China
ISBN 978 1 83869 0458

Managing Director, Publishing Piers Pickard
Associate Publisher Robin Barton
Commissioning Editor Nora Rawn
Art Director Daniel Di Paolo, Kerry Rubenstein
Print Production Nigel Longuet
© Lonely Planet 2020
© photographers as indicated 2020
Illustrations © Lauren Crow unless otherwise indicated

Contributors: Alexis Averbuck, Blane Bachelor, James Bainbridge, Rhoda Belleza, Celeste Brash, Morgan Davies, Bailey Freeman, Sarah Gilbert, Bridget Gleeson, Carolyn Heller, Anita Isalska, Virginia Jealous, Lusinetta Winnie Kormon, Su-Yee Lin, Natalie Meade, Meher Mirza, Etain O'Carroll, Jasmin Paris, Elizabeth Paulson, Monique Perrin, Robert Reid, Andrea Schulte-Peevers, Zuzanna Sitek, Zachary Small, Helena Smith, Gloria Steinem, Valerie Stimac, Anne Thériault, Tasmin Waby, Kerry Walker, Luke Waterson, Layla West, Tony Wheeler, Aman Williams, Barbara Woolsey

Lonely Planet Offices

Australia
The Malt Store, Level 3,
551 Swanston St, Carlton, Victoria 3053
T: 03 8379 8000

USA
Suite 208, 155 Filbert Street,
Oakland, CA 94607
T: 510 250 6400

Ireland
Digital Depot, Roe Lane (Off Thomas Street)
The Digital Hub,
Dublin 8, D08 TCV4

Europe
240 Blackfriars Rd,
London SE1 8NW
T: 020 3771 5100

STAY IN TOUCH lonelyplanet.com/contact

Cover illustrations: © Lauren Crow; © Danussa / Shutterstock; © Canicula / Shutterstock;
© Terpsychore / Shutterstock